The Book that Shows How to Buy Quality Printing Profitably

101 WAYS TO SAVE MONEY ON ALL YOUR PRINTING

Third Printing

by Edmund J. Gross

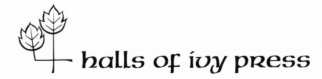

halls of ivy press

Library of Congress Catalog Card Number 70-138406

Standard Book Number 0-912256-02-8

Published by Halls of Ivy Press, 13050 Raymer Street, North Hollywood, CA 91605
PRINTED IN U.S.A.

FOREWORD

Each year thousands of dollars are needlessly added to the cost of producing printed matter. With a little forethought in preparation much of it could have been saved.

The helpful suggestions in this book are the result of 35 years in the Graphic Arts field. They will help you to save many dollars and moments of frustration when buying printing.

The prime point to remember at all times when you purchase printing is:

The more clearly you show your printer what you want the less you'll pay for the job and get a finished piece closer to what you have in mind. You will also eliminate the chance of mistakes and added expense for having to do the job over.

An investment in knowledge always pays
the best interest.

     —Ben Franklin, Printer

PREFACE

This book should be helpful to anyone who has ever ordered or has the need to order printing now or at some time in the future.

Businessmen use the most printing and, therefore, will find this book invaluable. However, most individuals will have dealings with a printer or engraver at some time during their lifetime. If you are active in your church or organization, you could very well find yourself handling an occasional order for some form of printed matter. This book can provide many valuable pointers to guide you in buying printing. It will help you better understand the requirements of ordering and show you ways to save time and money and prevent frustration.

The Glossary at the back of this book has been written to clarify all printing terms appearing in the book. You will find it an indispensible aid toward further understanding the vast printing field.

Keep this book handy—refer to it often—study the individual chapters on how they apply to each phase of a final printed job. Even if you've been ordering printed material most of your life you'll find it very helpful.

A penny saved is a penny earned.
—Ben Franklin, Printer

TABLE OF CONTENTS

Drive thy Business, or it will drive thee.
—Ben Franklin, Printer

CHAPTER 1

The Importance of Camera-Ready Artwork

What is Camera-Ready Art? It is usually one piece of artboard with all the elements (type, photos, drawings, borders, company name, etc.) pasted in the exact position they will appear on a finished printed piece. This artboard is placed on the copy holder of a printer's or engraver's camera and copied onto a negative which is used to make an offset plate or an engraving for letterpress printing.

Instead of the printer or engraver having to shoot several pieces of copy (type, headlines, photos, drawings, slogans, name and address lines, etc.), he shoots only one or two pieces of copy of the entire artwork with all the elements pasted in position. You can readily see why the cost would immediately come down when several camera shots are eliminated.

The next step in savings is the elimination of negative strip-ins of these same elements. If these elements are not on one board as in camera-ready art, the printer or engraver has to strip each negative onto what is called a "flat." This is a piece of orange opaque enamel paper. This type paper is used to prevent light from going through it. After they are taped into their proper positions, the areas of the negatives that are to print must be opened up so they can be exposed to the plate. This costly operation is called "stripping" which can be greatly avoided with camera-ready artwork.

HOW CAMERA-READY ARTWORK CAN SAVE YOU MONEY

More money can be saved in offset printing with camera-ready artwork than in any single phase of the printing process other than gang printing. Consider the cost of preparing a simple catalog sheet to be printed on 1 side in 2 colors of ink (color and black).

Here is a comparative cost analysis of camera-ready art vs non-camera-ready art:

CAMERA-READY ART FURNISHED

Preparation Costs for
Pasteup (includes type-
setting, photograph and
pasteup) _ _ _ _ _ _ _ _ _ _ _ _ _ _ _ $75.00

Photostat for Reverse
Heading _ _ _ _ _ _ _ _ _ _ _ _ _ _ _ _ 3.00

Negatives and Plates
for small offset press
(Multi type) _ _ _ _ _ _ _ _ _ _ _ _ 10.00

Total _ _ _ _ $88.00

ARTWORK FURNISHED IN SEPARATE PIECES

Preparation Costs
(includes typesetting
and photograph) _ _ _ _ _ _ _ _ _ _ $66.00

Negatives of various ele-
ments (type, photo, signa-
ture, reverse headline, etc.)   20.00

Stripping Negatives _ _ _ _ _ _ _ _ 20.00

2 Plates for Small Press _ _ _ _ _ _ 5.00

Total _ _ _ _ $105.00

Less Camera-Ready Art Method 88.00

YOU SAVE _ _ _ _ _ _ $ 17.00

(Note—the above costs are based on having clean copy and a working layout to follow. Prices may vary throughout the country but the comparision shown here will be proportionately the same for the same amount of work involved.)

Having all the elements (type, artwork, photos, borders, etc.) on one board not only cuts costs but also prevents them from being lost or damaged. One large board is much easier to file than several small pieces.

Throughout this book you will discover many ways to plan your printing better for the printer. The more things you do prior to giving him a go-ahead with your work, the more money you'll save.

This fictitious layout illustrates the job described on the opposite page. The two headlines and the company logo would be printed in color — the balance of the job in black. This is a very simple job and is only presented to show cost comparison.

Not to oversee Workmen, is to leave them your Purse open.

—Ben Franklin, Printer

CHAPTER 2

Procedure to a Finished Job

The two charts below show the steps necessary to move a job from copy to customer or prospect. Most steps are similar for both offset and letterpress, the exception being in the need for engravings or plates.

The index in this book was set up using these charts for easy reference. Each chapter carries one of the boxes in its proper sequence from COPY TO MAILING. Some variation occurs to combine offset with letterpress procedures.

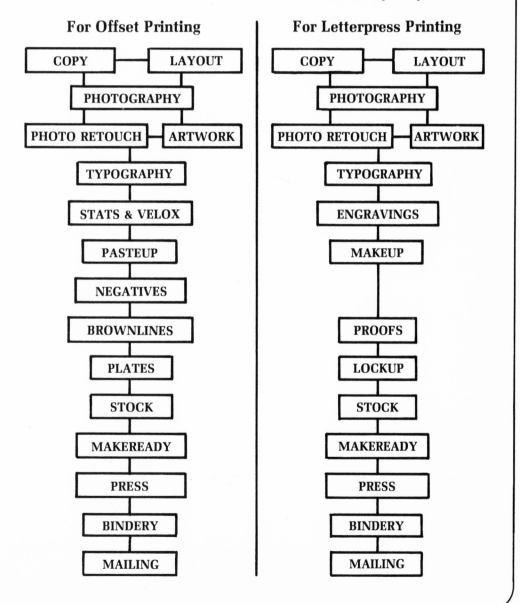

For Offset Printing	For Letterpress Printing
COPY — LAYOUT	COPY — LAYOUT
PHOTOGRAPHY	PHOTOGRAPHY
PHOTO RETOUCH — ARTWORK	PHOTO RETOUCH — ARTWORK
TYPOGRAPHY	TYPOGRAPHY
STATS & VELOX	ENGRAVINGS
PASTEUP	MAKEUP
NEGATIVES	
BROWNLINES	PROOFS
PLATES	LOCKUP
STOCK	STOCK
MAKEREADY	MAKEREADY
PRESS	PRESS
BINDERY	BINDERY
MAILING	MAILING

Haste makes waste.
                    —Ben Franklin, Printer

CHAPTER 3

How to Prepare Copy and Save Money

All the words that will appear on a printed piece or in an advertisement are considered to be copy. They include—

Headlines

Subheadlines

Captions for pictures

Body copy or text matter

Signatures and trademarks

Address and phone numbers

Slogans

Coupons

and any other words and phrases

pertinent to the printed piece.

How the copy is written, edited, organized and presented to the printer is essential if you want to save money and have a better printed job. Clearly written copy aids in making layouts since the printer or layout artist can more easily visualize which matter is most important. It also aids him in making a precise fitting of type. Follow the simple suggestions in this section when writing and preparing your copy and it will be to your monetary advantage.

1 Typewrite all copy (double spaced) whenever it is possible to do so. This enables the printer to visualize more rapidly the area the copy will fit into and the size of the type it can be set in. It also enables him to give you a more accurate estimate of the typesetting.

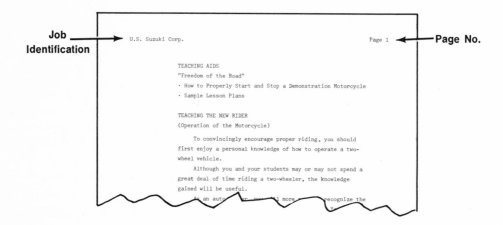

Job Identification → U.S. Suzuki Corp.   Page 1 ← Page No.

TEACHING AIDS
"Freedom of the Road"
· How to Properly Start and Stop a Demonstration Motorcycle
· Sample Lesson Plans

TEACHING THE NEW RIDER
(Operation of the Motorcycle)
    To convincingly encourage proper riding, you should
first enjoy a personal knowledge of how to operate a two-
wheel vehicle.
    Although you and your students may or may not spend a
great deal of time riding a two-wheeler, the knowledge
gained will be useful.

Allow a margin of one inch to one and one-half inches on the left hand side when typing your copy. This helps the printer to note his type styles, sizes and measurements as well as leaving space of any special instructions. (See above.) Use one side of the paper only.

2 **Always edit your copy** before submitting it to the printer. When it has to be done over several times for corrections and changes typesetting can run into a costly sum of money. This plus the fact that the more times type is handled the more chance there is of new errors. This means additional proofreading and added cost.

Editing copy before it is typeset entails more than just reading for typographical errors and misspelling. Such things as abbreviations should be watched—are they used uniformly throughout; watch those numbers—are they written out or used as figures*; and is punctuation and capitalization uniform? If the typesetter follows your copy without question and you have not "cleaned it up" you'll be paying for needless resetting.

*Figures from one through nine are written out, from 10 on they can be used as figures. If a figure is used as the first word in a sentence it should **always** be spelled out.

8

3   Whenever possible, prepare and submit all copy at one time. This will enable the printer to plan the work in a complete manner—not having to guess what is to come at a later date, and if it will fit into what has already been set. And, it will eliminate excuses for delay.

4   Always type your copy on a uniform size sheet of paper. Preferably 8 1/2 x 11" bond. It makes for easier handling and the chance for loss of copy is less.

5   Remember to number your copy, especially if there is a large number of pages. This tends to keep the copy in the proper sequence and helps to detect any misplaced pages.

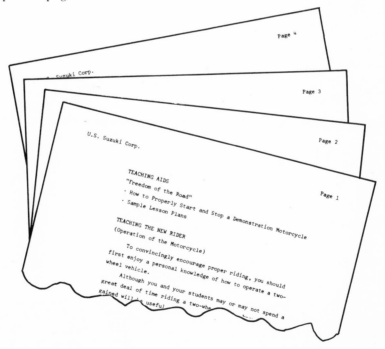

6   Where copy is to be set to fit a layout (and there should be a layout) or artwork, put all copy on standard size sheets and key the copy to your layout using numbers (1, 2, 3, etc.) or letters (A, B, C, etc.). Also indicate size of engravings, if any. It will be easier for the compositor to mark up without disturbing your artwork and will greatly expedite the production of the job.

HOW TO KEY YOUR COPY TO YOUR LAYOUT

COPY

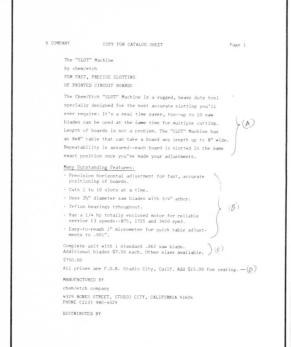

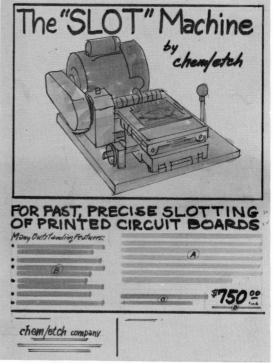

LAYOUT

CHAPTER 4

The Layout—
Blueprint for Your Printed Job

Most people ordering printing never provide their printer with a layout of what they have in mind for their finished job. They seem to think he has some magic power which will enable him to look at their copy (sometimes handed to him in very rough form) and immediately develop a printed job that will be an outstanding work of art. It just isn't done this way!

To produce a finished printed job requires the same methodical skill that an architect must use to guide a contractor in building a house. The printer or a layout man (his or yours) must consider all the basic ingredients required to "build" a printed piece. He must have clean, well edited copy, with headlines, subheadlines, body matter, captions, etc., all noted as outlined in Chapter 3 on Copy. Also, artwork and photos, if any, must be clearly identified.

From this he can visualize their importance and can begin roughing up ideas for layouts, carefully fitting all the pieces together like a jigsaw puzzle. There are certain basic rules he must follow to make a pleasing and effective layout. He must stay within the boundaries of standard paper sizes, use color wisely if required, keep in mind the printing method to be used (offset or letterpress), and plan for the bindery's requirements. He constantly works within limitations—all the while trying not to run up a bill you can't afford to pay. It takes real skill to be a good layout man.

Once you have a layout designed to make your copy "sell" you have a "blueprint" which can be followed to get a quality printed piece accurately done at no more money than some thrown-together mediocre printed job which would never "sell" your product or service.

There are many good books on layout at your library* that can be very helpful in guiding you in working with a printer or layout man. With some practice you can make "rough" layouts. These will often help you communicate more quickly with your printer and aid him in making finished layouts faster, easier and cheaper. Keep in mind that **he** supplies the creative talent to make your job "sell", so don't limit him to your ideas only. Let him have the freedom that creative people need to do their best for you by not confining him to this or that idea you might suggest. A frustrated layout man can never do his best for you. Too many limitations destroy his creative incentive.

*See books on Printing, Advertising and Commercial Art.

7   Always submit a layout with your copy. Have someone capable of making a good layout do one for you if you cannot do it yourself. It's worth the nominal fee usually charged for this service. After all, you wouldn't build a house without a blueprint. Nor should you start a printed piece without a layout. If your printer does not offer a layout service, check your telephone directory yellow pages for commercial artists or advertising services.

8   The "thumbnail" layout is the best way to go when you are working up layout ideas. They are made in a miniature size which is proportionate to the final size layout. Here are a few examples of "thumbnail" layouts to get you started.

These three thumbnail layouts illustrate the variety of ideas the layout man can create from copy for a simple catalog page.

This type of layout is a very rough form of visualizing a printed piece and is not recommended for the printer's use. It is essential to select one of the many "thumbnails" you rough out and prepare a more finished one as mentioned in the next item—with felt pens and in **full size**.

9 Felt pens of various sizes and colors make excellent full size layouts. Their strong colors leave little doubt as to the importance of type styles and weights. Here are a few simple black and white layouts made with these pens to give you an idea of what can be done and how easy it is for the printer to visualize what you have in mind.

10 Always make your final layout to the actual size you want the finished printed piece. There will be no room for argument if the printer has an accurately measured layout to follow. He'll also be able to determine the best paper size required for your particular job. However, before starting a layout, it is best to consult the printer about paper sizes.

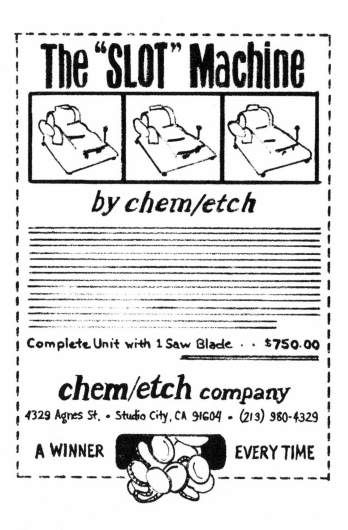

Actual size layout of a trade magazine ad which appeared in several publications.

CHAPTER 5

Choosing the Right Kind of Artwork for the Job

Not every printed piece or advertisement requires artwork. However, most do, to illustrate a product, catch the attention of a potential customer, or to emphasize some important point of the copy. If your particular job requires artwork, the following will help you in understanding the various types that are available to you. You should keep in mind that not all artists can do all types of artwork described here. Most artists specialize in one or a few mediums of art. There are artists who do nothing but airbrush photo retouching, for example. If you want to handle your own buying of artwork then search out the type of artist you need for a particular art medium and if he's good, stick with him. Usually, unless you are well aware of art quality, it is best to have your printer recommend someone or handle it for you, since he has access to many types of artists.

Choice of art for a specific printed job is determind by the following factors—

1. Budget for the printed piece
2. Type of layout
3. Particular subject to be advertised
4. How job is to be printed (offset or letterpress).

Here are the various types of art mediums you should know about.

LINE ART—Best detected by its black and white characteristics—lines or dots. Shades of gray are created by stippling, dry brushing on rough textures, close drawing of various line thicknesses and by Ben-Day screens. Here are most of the types of line art commonly used today:

BRUSH

PEN AND INK

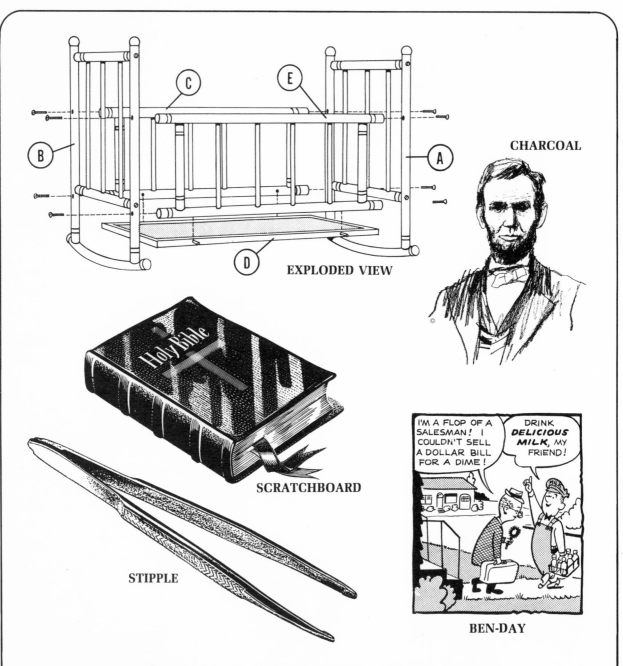

CHARCOAL

EXPLODED VIEW

SCRATCHBOARD

STIPPLE

BEN-DAY

Line art is cheaper than most other types of art unless it is highly intricate such as scratchboard. It is the best type of art medium to use for letterpress printing because of stock textures. For offset it always prints well on any type of stock. Most line artwork is done with pen and India ink.

WASH DRAWINGS—This type of art is basically transparent black water color painting with gray tones. Lamp black paint is diluted to various shades to create the gray tones. Reproduction of wash drawings must always be done by halftones to hold the gray areas. (See Chapter 12 on Negatives and Engravings.)

WASH DRAWING

OPAQUE ART—Another form of painting is the use of opaque water colors instead of transparent. Opaque paints come in various shades of gray—from white to black. Colors are not generally mixed but must be chosen from a wide array of shades. Being opaque they are somewhat like painting with oil paints.

The newest type of opaque paints are the acrylics. Like wash drawings, opaque art must be printed as a halftone to hold the gray tones. Again, they are best suited for offset printing unless you are using very slick paper stocks for letterpress.

OPAQUE ART

RETOUCHING PHOTOS—Photography is considered art in the printing trade. It is treated separately in this book for a specific reason—so you can better understand it and the many ways to save money when using it. Once photos have been shot and prints delivered to you by your photographer they should be carefully gone over by a qualified retouch artist or your printer to determine if retouching is required. In most cases, especially on products, some re-touching is necessary to bring out highlights, eliminate shadows and clean up blemishes picked up by the camera. Yes, even fingerprints, scratches and dents on products can be seen by the sensitive eye of the camera. Here is a typical photo before and after it was retouched.

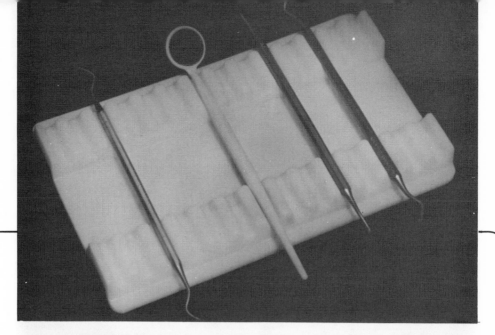

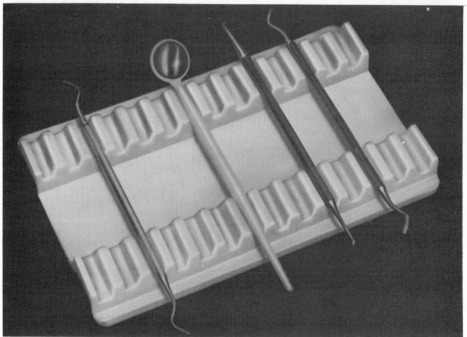

Retouching is done by airbrushing and hand touchup with brushes. It requires the skill of a top airbrush artist and should never be left to amatuers.

It is not a cheap art medium but if done properly it can make your products standout so they'll "sell."

Above shows photos of a product before and after airbrush retouching. Photo to right shows the airbrush artist at work.

Airbrush by Lou LaRose,
Graphic Artist, Van Nuys, CA.

19

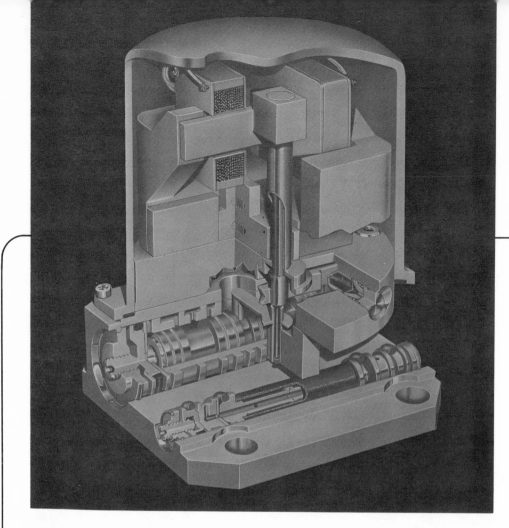

This highly detailed piece of art was produced by airbrush from only a blueprint. Where no product is available to photograph the artist must be able to read and work from blueprints to create an illustration. Airbrush rendering by Lou LaRose, Graphic Artist, Van Nuys, CA.

AIR BRUSH RENDERINGS—For that photographic look for products where great detail and sharpness are required on items such as instruments and fine products, air brush is the best method to use without actually photographing the item. The air brush artist starts from scratch to construct a product, sometimes only from blueprints. With careful skill he sprays various gray tones on an artboard to make a beautiful illustration that will be printed as a soft halftone on some fine quality paper. Air brush renderings can also be done in color.

Typical example of how art is commonly used in printed advertising are as follows:

LINE ART—Drawings of products, cutaway views, schematic views, exploded views, attention-getting spot drawings of people, situations and gimmicks, cartoons and scratchboard or woodcut technique for jewelry advertising and other luxury type products.

WASH OR OPAQUE DRAWINGS—Mostly used for fashion ads, furniture and similar type products. Also to give a feeling of photographic realism without an actual photo being used for products and backgrounds.

AIR BRUSH RENDERINGS—Mostly used for high quality mechanical renderings such as instruments and products that must have a true photographic look.

Always treat your artwork like it was money. Protect it with a sturdy cover and keep it well labeled and filed flat where it won't get damaged.

11 Always insist that all your artwork is returned to you from the printer once he is through with the job. You should keep a file and label all artwork for future use. Many times the artwork will represent a sizeable portion of the printed job. Having the artwork available is a definite advantage when a portion is needed for some other job. It's a simple matter to have a photostat or a neg and print made to use in another pasteup.

12 Here's a way to accumulate trademarks, company name and address lines, slogans, etc., at little or no cost for those RUSH jobs of pasteup. When you send out artwork to be shot for offset printing attach small pieces of trademarks and other line artwork to the edges of your job. Have these items shot along with your job making sure to leave sufficient cutting space around all items (one-half inch to one inch is best). Sometimes there will be no added cost for the difference in negative size. Most times the charge is only pennies more. You can keep these negs on file or gang them up for a print or two and have both negs and prints on file. There will be times when your artwork will be reduced or enlarged. This is especially good since you'll accumulate a variety of sizes of trademarks, etc., which are always handy to have on hand.

13 Where full photos are wanted, use Bourges white or gray overlay sheets to subdue the backgrounds when you want products or people to stand out. You can save the cost of retouching out backgrounds for very little money.

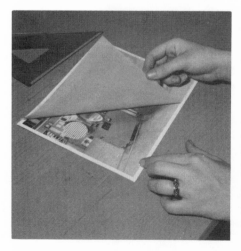 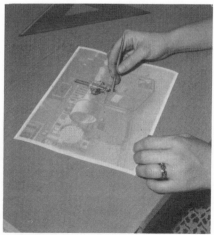 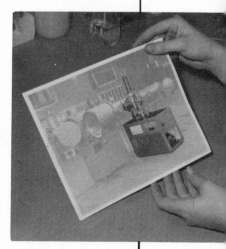

In the first picture the artist is attaching a piece of 30% white Bourges to a photograph. Next she carefully scrapes away areas where that portion of the picture is to show through. The final picture shows the finished result — important highlights of the photo in a subdued background.

Your art supply store has Bourges printed acetate overlay sheets in various percentages of white, gray and black. These can be attached to your mounted photo. You simply scrape away the coating for the subjects you want to appear. The remaining tone will subdue the background and give a very pleasing effect.

14 An ideal way to save money on artwork and pasteups is to borrow prepared work from your suppliers, manufacturers or non-competitors instead of running up costs of preparing new, yet similar ideas. Many times one of these firms has an idea you would like to adopt to your needs and they would be very willing to supply photostats of their artwork or photo print copies of their printing negatives for you to use with your own modifications. A letter of inquiry is usually all it will take to get an answer. Always offer to pay for negative or print costs—they're minimal. Here is an example of how such a mailing piece can be converted to other use:

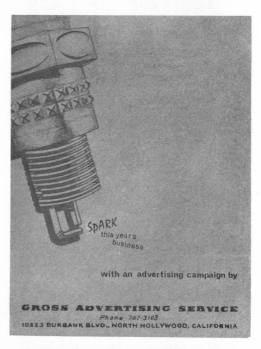

At left is original printed job. At right is new layout idea created from this original job.

15 When preparing artwork keep in mind that most engravers' and offset printers' cameras reduce to only five or six times original size. Therefore, if art is prepared for greater reductions than five or six times, there will be extra charges for further reduction since shooting will have to be done in steps. To accomplish an additional reduced size the cameraman must make a print of the first reduced negative and then reshoot it to a smaller size. Try to keep your original artwork within the five or six times reduction size. Also, the more steps, the greater the chance of lost detail especially where thin lines and spaces appear.

16

How to Outline Photos the Inexpensive Way—Eliminating backgrounds from photographs of products to be used in printed matter can be costly and time-consuming if left to the printer or if done on the negatives. It's also much more difficult to work on the reduced sizes when in negative form than on the original 8x10" photos. A shortcut to this costly method is to make a knockout mask over the original retouched or unretouched photo (see illustration). Plus saving money you will usually get a better result especially when the original is reduced a third or more in size.

First picture shows clear acetate attached to photo. Next the artist is applying Zip-a-Tone to the acetate. Outlining the product by cutting away the unwanted Zip-a-Tone is shown in the third picture. Completed mask is shown in the last picture.

Photos taken at Gross Advertising Service. North Hollywood, CA.

Several materials on the market can be used to knockout backgrounds. A sheet of red Zip-a-Tone with self-adhesive can be used by first placing a sheet of .005" clear acetate over the photo and attaching the acetate at the top with scotch or masking tape. Cut a large enough piece of red Zip-a-Tone sheet and place on acetate to fully cover the area you want to reproduce. Carefully rub this down with the flat of your thumb nail. Next with an X-Acto type pointed knive cut around the area you want to print. After cutting lift off the Zip-a-Tone from the area surrounding your subject. This will leave a red mask of what you want to print. Burnish the remaining Zip-a-Tone for permanence. To clean up the wax or glue left by the removed Zip-a-Tone, use rubber cement thinner on a piece of soft tissue or cloth.

When you give this photo with its knockout mask to the printer or engraver he will shoot a halftone negative of the photo and a line negative of the mask. By placing the line negative (with its clear window over the halftone negative he will automatically drop out any background making an outlined engraving or offset plate of your product.

Other products that are recommended for making knockout masks are: Amberlith by Ulano Products and Separon by Separon Company. Each of these color masking sheets come already mounted on clear acetate. You simply mount the entire sheet over the photo and cut away the areas you don't want. Most larger art stores carry one or more of the above mentioned items.

17 A low cost way to restore a trademark that may be lost or damaged from years of use is to have a large photostat (three or four times upsize) made of the best copy of the trademark you can find. An artist can usually touchup this photostat within a minimal amount of time. For only a few dollars you now have a good clean, up-to-date trademark that, if protected, will serve you for many more years.

18 Where type is to be used on photos over black or gray background areas, both time and money can be saved by using transfer type which comes as proofs on acetate sheets. These complete type fonts can be purchased in art supply stores, some drafting equipment stores and in larger stationery stores.

First, mount the photo to a piece of chipboard or similar cardboard with rubber cement. Be certain photo is smoothly mounted. Next, attach a piece of clear acetate .005" to the top of the photo. On this clear acetate sheet you will place your transfer letters, rubbing them off their sheet one at a time after carefully lining them up. An easy way to line them up is to draw a pen line on a separate sheet of tracing paper (one you can see through) and place it between the photo and acetate. Adjust the tracing paper to the desired position you want the words to appear. Now, one by one, rub off the letters from their master sheet onto the clear acetate until you complete the words you want.

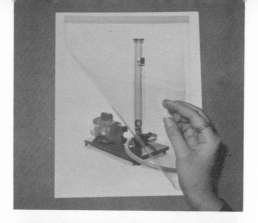

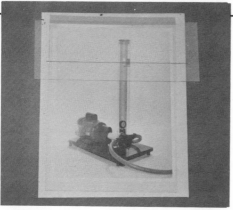

Top picture shows clear acetate attached to photo. A piece of tracing paper with ruled line is shown inserted between acetate and photo. In the third picture transfer type is carefully applied to acetate using the ruled line as a guide. After all the words are down the ruled paper is removed as seen in the bottom picture.

The photo can now be shot as a halftone without the need for special typesetting, film negative and film positives usually required to combine type with photos. Note—Use black type on white or light gray areas, white type on dark gray or black areas. (See pointers on Typography—Reverses—for type styles to use for best reproduction.)

How to Scale a Photograph

Attach a tissue overlay to your photograph.

With a fine felt pen mark the area of the photograph you want printed.

Draw a diagonal line to the corners of the cropped area.

Measure the width of the area on your layout or pasteup where photograph is to fit. Draw a line from the edge of the square to the diagonal line. The distance from the end of this line to the bottom of the square is the height.

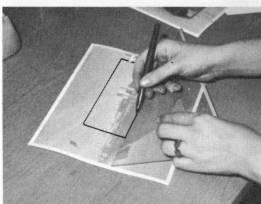

CHAPTER 6

How to Get More Out of Your Photos

It is not our purpose in this chapter to tell you how to photograph subjects, but rather to help you get more out of your photos. It's always best to seek out the services of a professional commercial photographer when you want good quality photos to sell your products or services.

Good professional photography can actually save you money in the long run. Since most photos should be retouched by an airbrush artist, much money can be saved when there is good detail and definition of subjects, especially when it comes to machinery, tools and hardware. Only the professional can get the results you need for photographs that will reproduce on printed literature.

There are some instances when the Polaroid camera is most helpful. An example of this is the sales bulletin or quickie catalog for in-plant use. Besides being inexpensive, the Polaroid offers immediate results ready for the printing press.

Here are several suggestions on how to properly handle photographs, work with a photographer and, in general, get more from your photo budget.

19   Always shoot two or more photos when you have it done professionally. The first shot usually runs from $10 to $15 (black and white) and each succeeding shot costs from $5 to $10.00. Sometimes another view of a product is usually worth the added cost. It could well make the difference in producing a more effective ad or sales sheet.

TYPICAL STOCK PHOTOS.

Stock photos courtesy of
North Hollywood Photo, North Hollywood, CA.

20   Stock photo services are an excellent way to get difficult shots without the high cost of good photography. Check your local yellow pages for photographers who handle stock photos. Always explain how you intend to use them. You pay in proportion to use of the photo. For local advertising use their cost is very nominal.

21   A Polaroid camera can be of tremendous help in making comprehensive layouts before money need be invested in final professional photography. Shoot a few black and white Polaroid shots you feel would look good on your layout and have them photostated to larger sizes to fit—even flopped to face the opposite way. The stats can be cropped, trimmed or angled to make your layouts interesting. These layouts will also help guide a photographer in final shooting.

An example of what happens to a photograph when someone has carelessly written on its reverse side.

22 Never write on the back of a photograph with a pencil or pen that will press through the picture. If you must write on a photo, always use a felt pen. Better still, put all instructions and key information on a separate piece of paper and attach to the back of the photo with tape. Impression marks can be difficult to remove (if not impossible) when photos are made into halftones for printing.

Artist applying rubber cement to back of photograph and mounting board. Next artist is positioning cemented photo to cemented board using a clean piece of paper between them. Finally paper is being removed and photo is carefully smoothed to board.

23 To mount photographs for permanent preservation use dry mounting tissue. This requires a special press which most photographers have. Where photos are wanted for temporary display or as art for pasteup, then rubber cement can be used. It should be applied to both surfaces—the back of the photo and the front of the mounting board—then left to dry. After drying they should then be mounted to the board using a clean piece of paper between the photo and the board until position is attained. Carefully rub down a contacted corner or top edge of photo, then slide out the paper while rubbing down photo. With a rubber cement pickup eraser rub off any access rubber cement from board around the photo.

The proper way to mark a photo for cropping is shown at left. Portion of photo seen below is incorrect method of cropping.

24 Photographs should **never** be cut down to size with scissors. This leaves no area for scale or crop marks and does not allow the printer or engraver space for bleeds or to clean edges. Always leave your photos full size.

CHAPTER 7

Selecting the Best Typeface for Your Printing

Pick up any newspaper or magazine and you'll see the many styles of type available. All newspapers, magazines and books are set by machine—Linotype, Monotype, Ludlow and now, the newest electronic typesetting equipment which does it photographically.

However, the average job printer still uses hand set type for much of his every day work. Large typesetting jobs are sent out to typesetting firms if the printer does not have a linotype machine on which to set them. Electronic

Photos courtesy of Merganthaler Linotype Co., Plainview, NY.

(Left) The Elektron II Linotype machine used to set "hot metal" type in slug form. (Right) This is the latest model of computer typesetting equipment known as the Linotron 505 System. It sets type photographically from coded tape to produce "cold type" in film form. Paper prints are made from these negatives or positives and are used for pasteup.

typesetting equipment is and will be beyond the financial reach of small printers for many years to come.

Hand set type is made up of several pieces of each letter of the alphabet (CAPS, lower case and figures) into what is called a font of type.

A font of 18 point Stymie Black Type.

These fonts are placed in type cases having receptacles for each letter or figure. A highly skilled craftsman known as a compositor sets the type, letter-by-letter, into a composing stick adding the proper spaces between words and lines.

The type is then taken from the composing stick and placed into a galley where the lines are further spaced out to fit a given area of copy on a layout. From there it can be printed direct by letterpress or it can be repro proofed for use on pasteups for offset printing.

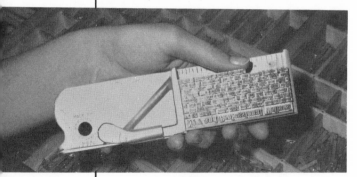

Composing stick with type.

Compositor setting type from case.
Photo taken at Art Page Typesetting, Glendale, CA.

Made up galley of type ready for proofing.

Type locked in chase ready for letterpress printing.

Photo from American Type Founders' brochure.

Very fine work can be created with hand set type if it is kept in good condition. Since most printers print directly from their type, you may find the quality lacking since many letters, being used over and over, get nicked and worn. For top quality typesetting it is best to have hand set type set by a reputable typesetting firm who keeps its type in perfect condition. They do not print from it but pull repro proofs for pasteup use which can be used for offset printing or for engravings.

Typositor shown pulling a repro proof of a type setup.

No. 3ST Pen-Knife. Clips to pocket. "See-Thru" cap reveals blade. Gold finish metal barrel. Complete with No. 10 blade. Length closed is 5¼.

No. 66g All Purpose Pocket Slide-Knife Set. Contains knife handle and two blades.

No. 66 Pocket Slide-Knife on Cards with 1 blade (1 dozen cards to box).

No. 7-kp Knife-Pencil Combination. Pencil on one end. See-thru cap reveals blade on other end.

X-ACTO Set Display No. SDX-1970. Contains 7 of X-Acto's best selling sets. Sets are clearly numbered and priced to make selection and selling easy. Display measures 17 wide x 10 deep x 23 high and weighs approximately 20 pounds.

Optical Corporation

BUSHNELL EXPO Extra Power BINOCULAR

A unique focus system eliminates the tricky adjustment for sharp, clear picture. Field of view 394 feet at 1000 yards. 8 Power with 30mm light gathering lens. Weighs only 12 ounces. Neck strap and lens cover included. Fiberglass construction. Shockproof, waterproof. Packed in polystyrene display box with clear plastic cover and protective sleeve. Master Pack — 12 units in crisp white on black self-merchandising display.

KEY RING COMPASS

Snapshooter Camera Co.

Individually boxed, these cameras are suitable for mailing. Included with each camera is a No. 126 Cartridge (12 exposures) of black and white film, wrist strap and instruction sheet. This camera is made in U.S.A. Color film may also be used with this camera. It's a new and exciting value. Put them on a counter and watch them go. It will also build film sales.

REPRO PROOF

Photo taken at Art Page Typesetting, Glendale, CA.

Here are a few ideas which were created with hand set type, rules and ornaments only:

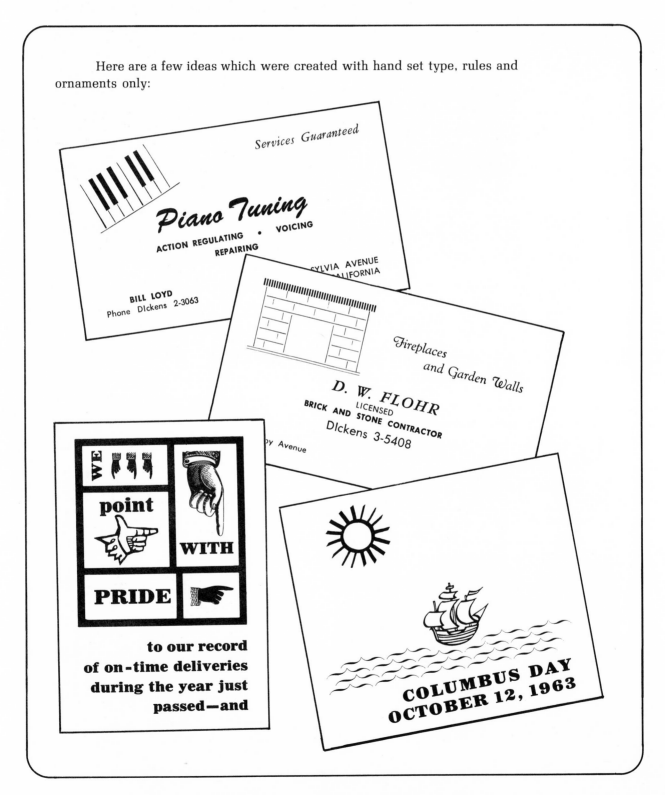

The newest members to the typesetting trade are the photo composing machines. They set type photographically from film fonts or grids depending upon the type of equipment being used. Some of the photo typesetting machines set body type (6 point to 14 point) and others set display sizes (18 points and up).

Shown here is a Phototypositor which sets display lines in a variety of sizes, widths, heights and slants through the use of distortion lenses. From a single negative film strip (font) of type, 2800 variations can be achieved. A few of the many typesetting possibilities of this unique machine are shown here:

Body type does not require the variations that display type does for attention-getting headlines. Instead, body or text matter needs the speed of getting the job done faster and better at less cost. With computerized typesetting machines it's now possible to set an entire newspaper page from a programmed tape produced by skilled keyboard operators in a matter of only a few minutes. The computor produces a finished film negative, or film positive or paper print ready for whatever use the printer requires.

Shown here is the Alphatype computor system in operation.

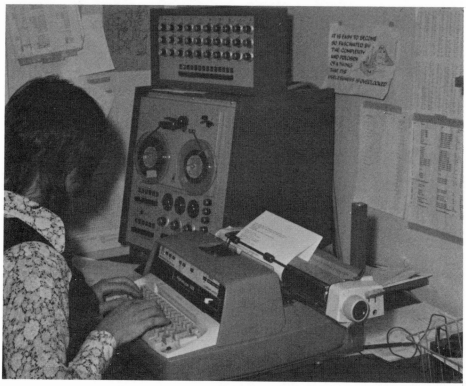

Photo taken at Macson Printing & Lithography, Glendale, CA.

In this section are many pointers which explain the best way to handle your typesetting requirements, type styles to use for best results, and general shortcuts in ordering type. All ideas are given with the thought of saving you money, time and frustration.

Carefully read through this entire section and also the section on COPY. In the COPY section you will find many ideas which will help you prepare work properly for the typesetter.

25   Every trade has its own terminology and the printing trade is no exception. Yet, day after day, people dealing with printers fail to use the terms of the trade. How simple it would be if they did. Specifying type is only one example of the importance of using printing terminology. Since typesetters can only set line lengths in picas and half-picas it makes sense to call out these measures in their proper language. Measures indicated in inches or fractions of inches make unnecessary work for printers and even with the extra work of converting to picas, there is no guarantee the measure will be accurate.

For example, if you specify a line length of 3-7/16", the printer will have to convert to 20-1/2 picas. This is as close as he can set to your measure. This portion of a printer's rule shows the comparison of picas and inches.

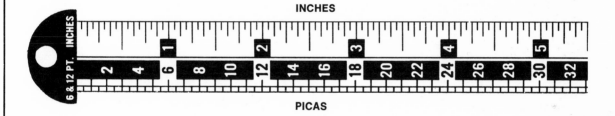

Using printer's terms can simplify character counting and make copy fitting more accurate. It would be wise to purchase a printer's pica rule at an art store or printer's supply house. You'll find it useful for many other purposes especially in proportioning photos and artwork.

26   If you are planning a booklet or catalog that will require a considerable amount of the same type face, first select a suitable one from your printer or typesetter. Next make a measure of the characters that can be set in the length of line you have decided to use. Then type all your copy with the same number of characters to the line that you will have in the type line selected. This can save a tremendous amount of time and money on your part and the typesetter's and both of you will know in advance how many lines of type will be needed for the job.

27   When having type set, ask your printer or typesetter to hold the type for 90 days before "killing" the forms. In some cases there may be a token storage charge but it could be worth many dollars in savings over having to reset the type. When type is held, corrections can be added, words or lines deleted, and paragraphs can be rearranged.

28 Watch those Reverses when using type that could fill in and ruin a good ad or piece of literature.

Always use a type that is strong enough so that when reversed the letters are easy to read. Types in the Gothic family always print best in reverse. Some Romans can be used if the serifs and the light elements are not too fine. Square serifs are best. This illustration shows the various characteristics of a piece of Roman type as compared to Gothic type.

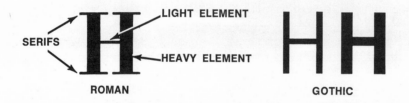

Some Roman style types which can be used successfully in reverses are Stymie Medium, Stymie Bold and Extra Bold, Bookman, Craw Clarendon and Clarendon Book, Cheltenham in all weights, Hellenic Wide and Melior. Reverses tend to fill more readily on small presses of the Multilith type because there is less ink control and coverage than on the larger presses.

29 Where there are many pages of tabular or text matter such as in publications it is best to have type set and made up according to a layout provided from galley proofs. Exact spacing can be added before a repro proof is made for pasteup.

30 On book jobs where you have a number of photos and price is a factor, try to have the halftones made the same width as the width of your type column. For example, on an 8 1/2 x 11" page having three columns of type 13 picas wide, it would be better to have your halftones made the same column width in order to avoid the costly runarounds and narrow measures. These are expensive and time consuming. Where photos are to cover two or three columns be certain to allow "gutter" space between columns. (See next page.)

Exit light has self-contained battery

Dewlight is an exit light with a self - contained nickel cadmium battery for continuous operation in the event of power failure, fire or other emergencies.

The built-in, solid-state power cell protector operates off existing 115v, 60-cycle power supply during normal conditions. However, in the event of a power failure, the controller automatically switches to the

Family Style meat loaf is prepared from quality lean ground beef blended with all the proper seasonings and ingredients.

The product is packaged in a

foil-lined container that can be placed directly into the oven for baking.

The above illustrates why it is more costly to set type around a picture. Below is shown simpler, less costly methods of setting type in columns where pictures are required.

31 Very often, where large types are to be used such as on display cards, etc., considerable money can be saved by setting the job in smaller size types on a linotype machine and blowing up the reproduction proofs by photostat. Extreme care must be taken that the printer's type is in excellent condition and reproduces well. Imperfections will show up when enlarged. It is best to confine your blow ups to not over two times original size. Linotype sizes beyond 14 points tend to be pitted and require a large amount of touch-up on the repros. But even by doubling the sizes—8, 10, 12 and 14 point—you will have type 16, 20, 24 and 28 point. These sizes (actually 14, 18, 24 and 30 point) in type would cost from two to three times as much as linotype if set by hand or on a photo typesetting machine.

32 For a minimal charge you can have your printer or engraver put a screen behind the negatives shot of large boldface types. Besides toning down over-powering black face types, you will get a completely different effect. Often-times it eliminates the need to reset type in a lighter or different face. It also allows you to use the type face of your choice simply by reducing its strength. Other special effects can be had by using screens other than unnoticeable dot patterns. There are lines, circles, crosshatches, wavy lines, brick patterns and cloth patterns to select from.

33 On jobs requiring a **considerable amount** of typesetting (booklets, books, catalogs) it will pay you to have it set by a professional typesetting house. If the printer has it set by a type house it would cost you more since he would have to mark up a profit for handling it. Further savings can be realized if you have all your corrections and alterations done while the type is still at the type house. Then when the printer gets the type it is ready for him to make up and print. Remember, the more handling he has to do for you the more he must charge for his time and service. Also, you own the type when you have it set at a type house. You will have to pay for the metal, but you can return it for credit when the printing job is completed.

34 Occasionally there is a need for using the same type setup on various pieces of literature. If this is necessary, have the type set a size or two larger (when space warrants) with appropriate measures to compensate for future reductions. When repro proofs are reduced you'll have sharp, clear typography for those other pieces of printed matter. Your only real restriction is the length limit of the type setup. For example: Type set in 14 points, 30 picas long will reduce to the following pica lengths if these point sizes are desired:

> If reduced to 12 point type the length will be 25 1/2 picas;
> If reduced to 10 point type the length will be 21 1/2 picas;
> If reduced to 8 point type the length will be 17 picas;
> If reduced to 6 point type the length will be 13 picas.

Bear in mind that as type reduces in size it also reduces in strength or weight. Lightface type should be avoided if extreme reductions are to be made. It is wise to stay with medium and bold weight types for best reductions. The above chart is only a guide to show the approximate finished lengths. Other variations may be made. A good proportion rule will help you determine various reductions.

35 When having linotype set keep line measures within 30 picas whenever possible to do so. "Split" slug setting costs more money. It is better to have more columns of type set less than 30 picas than to set long lines over 30 picas. When setting lines over 30 picas the typesetter must divide the new length into two equal parts and set two slugs instead of one. Example—A line to be set 32 picas must be set on two slugs 16 picas each, sawed to measure and butted together before it can be repro proofed. Besides being more costly, readability is lessened with long lines.

These two 16-pica slugs must be cast separately, sawed to measure and butted together to make a 32-pica line.

A 30-pica Linotype slug.

36 Display type (sizes over 14 points) and body or text type (sizes 14 points and smaller) should be typed on separate sheets of paper if there is a reasonable quantity of type to be set. Since the two classes of type are composed in different departments, the work can be carried on in two different places at the same time. This increases speed in production especially if there is a tight schedule of delivery.

37 Justified type set in narrow measures can increase your typesetting cost and lower the quality of the work. In narrow measures natural breaks cause some lines to be widely spaced and others to be to tight. Both tight and wide lines look bad and are very costly to set. If narrow measures cannot be avoided then use smaller or condensed type faces. The best solution to the problem is to specify "flush left, ragged right" composition. The job will look better and readability will greatly improve. Also you will save considerable money if there is any great amount of narrow measure type to be set.

Another important factor for this year's sales is the cadre of experienced salesmen which has been built up by the industry. This will be highly significant for the man-

JUSTIFIED

Another important factor for this year's sales is the cadre of experienced sales- men which has been built up by the industry. This will be highly significant for the

FLUSH LEFT

CHAPTER 8

The Many Uses of Photostats, Negatives and Prints

Too few people ordering printing realize the value of the **photostat** as a means of keeping type and artwork all on one piece of artboard. They very rarely think of using them. Yet commercial artists and art departments of advertising agencies regularly use them to facilitate pasteups.

Basically a photostat is a negative print made of an original piece of copy—mostly repro proofed type and line artwork. Instead of getting a negative on film, you get it on paper—forward (right reading) not backward as on film negatives. This paper negative is ideal for reverse blocks (white letters on black background). However, if you want your photostat like the original copy (black on white background) you will need an additional (positive) photostat made of your negative stat.

Where reductions and enlargements are needed as a positive, the photostat is ideal. Cost in not prohibitive. There is usually a minimum charge of $2 or $3 for a single negative and a very small additional charge for the positive copy. And, of course, the more copies you order the cheaper the rate gets. One thing you must be very careful of when ordering photostats is that the photostater knows that you want the finished stat for **reproduction use.** If he is not told this he is likely to give you a finished stat with the black looking gray or with a gray (muddied) background. Your stats must be sharp black and white to reproduce as camera-ready art for printing.

Film Negatives and Prints—If you have an engraver or litho plate service in your area, it will pay you to use his services instead of the photostater. The photostater is limited to black and white line work for reproduction and sometimes may lack the facilities or knowhow to do **reproduction type** negatives and positives. This is where the engraver's camera or that of a litho plate service can be most useful. Even your printer who does your offset work might be willing to furnish you with reproducible prints for your pasteups.

These graphic arts specialists are equipped for line work (type and artwork) and halftones. You will need their services at some time if you use photographs or wash and opaque art on your pasteups. See Chapter 5—Artwork for complete details on all types of artwork.

Whenever you use photographs on your printed matter you should consider the use of screened **velox** prints. Since you will have to pay for a halftone negative of your photo to have it printed, it is just as easy to have it made into a velox print for your pasteup.

The halftone negative is shot as usual with an appropriate screen (dots per inch). Instead of the printer stripping in the halftone negative with your line work negative in the position you've indicated, he provides you with a paper print of the screened negative. You cut out and paste this "Velox" print onto your artboard with your type and line artwork. You then have camera-ready "line" copy of your entire page or job. The screen in the Velox is considered line art because the dots will shoot as such being large and small to provide the various gray tones.

There's an important thing to remember when ordering Veloxes. That is, don't order the screen too fine, or the printer's camera won't be able to re-shoot it as good clean line art. It is best to work between 100 and 120 line screens for sharpest reproduction. We recommend a 110 line screen for general use. Of course, newspaper ads if printed by letterpress, require a 65 line screen—very coarse. Some newspapers are now converting to offset printing and will accept the 110 line screens. Always check their mechanical requirements before ordering your screens.

Here is a 110 line Velox print of a photograph.

Velox print highly magnified showing dot structure.

The Velox print is especially economical when several photos are being used in a printing job. In catalogs they are real money savers. In this chapter you will find many valuable pointers on using Velox prints, negatives and prints and photostats.

38   **Extreme enlargements**—A handy way to make small size types into display type for sales presentations, display use, visual aids or posters, is to have a small (less expensive) type setup made and repro proofed. Next have these type proofs enlarged by photostat to many times up size. Photostat cameras generally enlarge two times up. The first enlargement you will get will be a negative. This is then reshot to a larger size (another 2 times or less) to make a positive print. This step up process can be repeated for another round of negs and prints if need be for extra large blowups—something that would have to be read from a great distance.

Automatic Reset Timer—
Heavy Duty Contactor
For fast, accurate repeat settings. Calibrated in seconds. All pre-wired. Simply plug into 220-volt line.

YOUR ORIGINAL COPY

Automatic Reset Timer—
Heavy Duty Contactor
For fast, accurate repeat settings. Calibrated in seconds. All pre-wired. Simply plug into 220-volt line.

2 TIMES UP — NEGATIVE

Automatic Reset Timer— Heavy Duty Contactor

For fast, accurate repeat settings. Calibrated in seconds. All pre-wired. Simply plug into 220-volt line.

ANOTHER 2 TIMES UP — POSITIVE

utomatic Reset Timer—
eavy Duty Contactor
or fast, accurate repeat settings. Cali-
rated in seconds. All pre-wired. Simply

STILL ANOTHER 2 TIMES UP — NEGATIVE

39   Save money on photo prints of artwork and type repros by requesting the cameraman or printer to gang as many negatives as possible on a print. Generally prints are very inexpensive, usually a dollar so a piece). You can then cut the prints apart and use them on your artwork or file them for future use. This eliminates the cost of an individual print for each negative. You can save anywhere from $1 or more per print by ganging your artwork and type repros in this manner.

ORIGINAL   FLOPPED PRINT

40 To make a photo or a piece of artwork look like a new item or to help it fit better into a layout, you can have the original shot to size and "flopped". The negative is placed emulsion side up so the finished print will face the opposite way. Care must be taken if there is any type on the artwork since it will read backwards. This method is one that can save money in not having to reshoot or redraw products.

41 It's no trick to separate colors when you want to reduce colored or tinted artwork or copy printed in more than one color to clean black and white art for reuse in new layouts. Most color separation can be done by photostat without the costly and time-consuming work of redrawing the artwork that is already printed in two colors. Stats made from drawings on graph paper can drop pastel graph lines. Illustrations show color before and after being color corrected.

Some colors will not separate too clearly, therefore, some touchup by an artist is necessary. However, it's still a lot cheaper than redoing original art.

ORIGINAL

TOUCHED UP PHOTOSTAT

42 For new jobs that require parts of previously printed material, time and money can be saved by having prints made of existing offset negatives. (Of course, the original jobs would have had to be printed by offset.) The prints you get can be used to create new layouts, thus saving the cost of resetting type for most of the new jobs. They can then be used for pasteup.

43 With the use of a distortion camera many variations of copy can be obtained. Proportions can be changed in width or in length without destroying the original copy layout. If you have a piece of copy such as an advertisement that is the right height but too wide for another publication or for use on a sales sheet, it is not necessary to have the artwork completely redone. You can avoid this expensive cost of art and typography by using a distortion camera. It will leave your ad intact while only changing the width to fit the new ad space. See example below. Many larger typesetting firms and photostat companies have distortion lenses on their cameras. Any nearby large city has several typesetting and photostat companies listed in the Yellow pages of the phonebook.

ORIGINAL AD

WIDER (Same Height)

TALLER (Same Width)

NARROWER (Same Height)

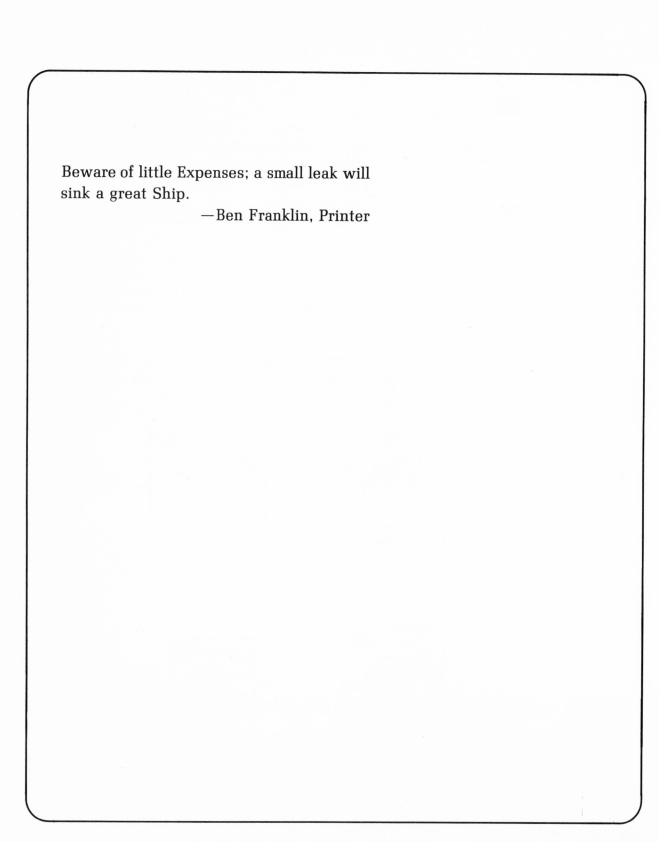

Beware of little Expenses; a small leak will sink a great Ship.

—Ben Franklin, Printer

CHAPTER 9

Pasteup Ideas to Save You Money

What is a Pasteup? This term appears quite often throughout this book. It is also called a "mechanical," "camera-ready art" or "copy." However, we refer to it chiefly as a **pasteup** or **camera-ready art.**

The illustration here shows a pasteup completely ready for the printer's or engraver's camera. It consists of type headline, subheadlines, body copy or text, velox print of photo, company signature and border, pasted in position on a sturdy piece of white illustration board. Note the corner marks to indicate the outside paper edges. This particular piece of work was pasted to be shot as same size. The size shown here is about one-half original size.

Why a Pasteup? The chief purpose of a pasteup is to have all the elements (type, photos, artwork, etc.) on one piece of illustration board to eliminate the need for several camera shots, stripping of negatives and additional opaquing.

The Advantages of Camera-Ready Pasteup are Many. There are certainly several more advantages than listed below, but these point out the most obvious ones:

1. It saves you money on negatives, opaquing, stripping and printing.

2. It keeps elements intact on one piece of artboard — prevents loss of photos, trademarks, artwork, etc.

3. It gives full visualization of the printed piece prior to printing.

4. It reduces the chance of errors because it allows for a final proofing of the job.

5. It is less costly and easier to make changes on camera-ready art than on negatives and plates.

6. It acts as a working guide and thus assures better printing results. Proper positioning of job on the stock is assured.

7. It always belongs to YOU—not to the printer!

Following the suggestions in this chapter on PASTEUP can be most helpful whether you do the pasteup or have someone do it for you. Many printers offer this service if they have pasteup artists available. Also most commercial artists do pasteups as part of their service.

Basic tools required for pasteup — Metal T-Square, 30°-60° Angle, Scissors, 6-H Pencil, Ruling Pen, Tweezers, No. 1 Pointed Brush, X-Acto Knife, Rubber Cement, Masking Tape and Printer's Pica Rule.

44 Always use a T-Square and Angle to line up copy when pasting up art for offset printing or engravings. Most printers won't take it upon themselves to realign the pasted up elements—they don't usually like to take the responsibility of altering your pasteup. If they do they will have to charge for this time.

45 Use only **light** blue pencil lines for guide lines and notations on your pasteup. These will drop out on the negative and thereby require no opaquing.

46 Never use tapes (masking, scotch, etc.) or mucilage type glues to hold elements in place on pasteups. **Always use Rubber Cement!** This will save many dollars in opaquing cost on negatives and allows for elements to be removed with rubber cement thinner when necessary without damaging the work.

47 When typewritten, Varitype or IBM Composer copy is used for pasteup it is wise to spray it very lightly several times with an acrylic solution so it will not smear in pasting up. This spray can be purchased in any art supply store.

48 Keep your copy flat. Cracks and folds photograph as black lines and cleaning up these unwanted marks can be very costly. Use a good sturdy type of artboard for pasteup.

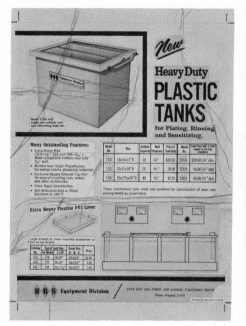 

This valuable piece of artwork was carelessly handled. The negative on the right was shot from it and will require much opaquing and touchup. It will also require a new halftone negative.

49 Always clean up your pasteups. Use an art gum eraser for lines and dirt marks, and a rubber cement pickup eraser for excess rubber cement that is left around pasted up elements. These spots make extra work for the printer which is chargeable. If you can't erase dirt marks, pencil marks, etc., then use an artist's white out paint and go over them with a good Number One pointed artist's brush. Also touch up pasteup edges of copy with the same white.

50 If you find it necessary to shoot newspaper copy and want to eliminate the printing on the back side, place a piece of black paper behind the newspaper copy. This will help subdue the printing on the opposite side and will help the cameraman do a better job of shooting the negatives. It will also eliminate much opaquing on the negative necessary to paint out pinholes and shadow lines from the opposite side.

51   A cover should be put over all photos and individual artwork and paste-ups. The covers should be labeled with instructions for the printer and for future filing purposes. One lost piece of artwork could mean many dollars down the drain.

52   If you do not use screen Velox prints of your photos then make "windows" for them on your pasteup. These windows enable the stripper to place the half-tones of your photos directly onto your line negatives and can save extra stripping and double burning costs. The window opens a clear area on the negative. Red Zip-a-Tone with adhesive backing is ideal to use for windows. It is available at art supply stores. Measure off the areas with a blue pencil where the photos are to appear. Place a piece of red Zip-a-Tone over and slightly beyond the marked areas. Rub down lightly so it will not lift. Then with your T-Square and angle cut away and remove the Zip-a-Tone that is beyond the blue lines. An X-Acto type pointed knife is ideal for cutting. Also a sharp single edge razor will do. After cutting rub the Zip-a-Tone down firmly against the artboard. Next scale your photos to fit the window areas and "key" photos and windows with letters or numbers—A, B, C, etc., or 1, 2, 3, etc.

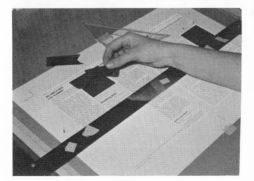

The artist first places red Zip-a-Tone over blue ruled areas where photos are to appear. She next cuts away and removes excess Zip-a-Tone. Final picture shows complete windows ready for square type halftones.

Printers...should be very careful how they omit a Figure or a Letter: For by such means sometimes a terrible Alteration is made in the Sense. I have heard, that once, in a new Edition of the Common Prayer, the following Sentence, **We shall all be changed in a Moment in the twinkling of an Eye**: by the Omission of a single Letter, became **We shall all be hanged in a Moment, etc.** to the no small Surprise of the first Congregation it was read to.

—Ben Franklin, Printer

CHAPTER 10

The Need for Proofs and Brownlines

The title of this chapter is quite self-explanatory. You can never check a job prior to printing too often. It is surprising how many little things are overlooked before the presses roll and how they stand out like sore thumbs when the first printed copies arrive.

If printing by **letterpress**, you have two opportunities to see proofs—first a galley proof should be requested for general reading, then a final makeup proof should be checked. Sometimes, it is even wise to have the printer furnish you a "press" proof, just before he starts the wheels turning. If you are convenient to his plant, it will pay you to rush over and see this last-minute proof. This is an opportunity to check the quality of the printing on your job, too.

Checking proofs for **offset** printing is somewhat different than for letterpress. You do have the same opportuntity to check type proofs—galleys and makeup proofs prior to repro proofs—plus an additional chance to check a "brownline" of the negatives before plates are made. This brownline is an inexpensive paper print of the entire job as it will appear on the offset plate. It usually appears in brown—however, some are blue or black. You should always request a brownline especially on complicated jobs and jobs with color.

One additional type of proof is the "Color Key." It is similar to the brownline only in that it is a print of the negative. The difference is that Color Key proofs are of clear film and come in various colors. With this ingenious system you see how your job will look in advance of printing. It is mostly used to indicate color and not generally used for grammatical or typographical proofreading as it is a more costly proof. Many printers and engravers can furnish Color Key proofs.

PROOFS

OFFICE HELP OR EXECUTIVES CAN
WEAR TUMMY TAMER ON THE JOB
MOTHERS, WEAR TUMMY TAMER AROUND
THE HOUSE AND REGAIN YOUR FIGURE

OVERCOME POOR POSTURE HABITS

We are all creatures of habit — some good and some bad. Poor posture, long considered one of man's worst habits, not only results in a protruding abdomen and thickened waistline but the strain placed upon the spine, back muscles and abdominal organs accounts for many of the aches and pains we all experience, in addition to that feeling of tiredness after a few hours of daily routine. Now, with **Tummy Tamer** it is possible for men, women and children to change that bad habit into a good habit and reduce waistlines down to any desired size. The **Tummy Tamer** not only helps you achieve this goal but, by working with your subconscious, does it without any great effort on your part.

NO UNCOMFORTABLE GARMENTS OR WEIGHTS

This compact, portable exercising device contains no bulky, cumbersome weights or rubber sweating devices. It can be worn over the clothing. It is made of nylon auto seat belt material with a high impact plastic case and weighs only 8 ounces. Figure consciousness is very important in our lives these days. We are constantly being told how important it is to our health to have good posture as well as maintaining good weight. But, we need help to achieve these health goals. That is where **Tummy Tamer** comes to the aid of all who are plagued with protruding abdomens, more commonly called "bulging stomachs," thickened waistlines, droopy shoulders and sagging backs.

EASY TO USE

Tummy Tamer is designed to give you the greatest possible result with the least amount of effort. Here is all you do: When you adjust the **Tummy Tamer** around your waist you will find it necessary to hold your abdomen in. If you relax or try to rest the stomach area against the **Tummy Tamer**, the belt mechanism will expand setting off a pleasant sounding buzzer. To stop the buzzer you must keep your abdomen pulled in. This automatically causes you to straighten up your spine and bring your shoulders back giving you a correct posture, which, in turn pulls in your waistline. Over a period of time this becomes a reflex action on your part because the knowledge of the buzzer sounding when you relax against the belt is registered on your subconscious. This, in turn, develops into a memory reflex which helps you stand up straight without being aware that you are doing so. Even when you are not wearing the belt you will subconsciously maintain the posture because the reflex has been built up.

WEAR IT ANYTIME, ANYWHERE

The **Tummy Tamer** can be worn for any length of time depending on how quickly you want your figure trimming results. A minimum of 10 minutes to one-half hour a day is recommended. The **Tummy**

CALENDARS MAGAZINES and NEWSPAPERS GREETING CARDS
SALES PROMOTION DISPLAYS

A WONDERFUL OPPORTUNITY FOR YOUR CHILD.

Think of the joy of possibly seeing your child's photo in a magazine, newspaper, calendar or other advertisement. Think of all the pleasures, pride and happiness it could bring to your family and your child.

THIS OPPORTUNITY CAN BE YOURS!

Hundreds of advertisers, large and small firms, publishers and advertising agencies through the country use children's photos. They are constantly looking for appealing, eye-catching new faces, situations, unusual types and poses that can be used for advertising and publicity purposes.

It does not matter if your child is not "the cutest" or "the prettiest," because an advertiser often needs a photo of a baby or child that has a "personality" that shows in the picture . . . pictures with surprised looks, tears, silly grins, etc. are also the pictures that are selected.

Give yourself the opportunity to have your child's photo printed in the next ADVERTISERS REGISTER!

Additional calendars as shown in BONUS #3 are available for $1.00 each, if made from the same photo. 6 additional Calendars, only $4.00. Only the photo you have already submitted is needed.

Your child's photo will be mounted and returned to you in this specially designed Golden Good-Luck Photo Calendar 5½" x 8½" in gold and grey. AN IDEAL GIFT!

You'll be proud to show this beautiful Award Certificate to your family and friends. It's authentic parchment, measures a full 5½" x 8½" and is ready for framing.

- New, smart, high-styled American-made snapshot camera. Takes excellent pictures.
- Simple, easy-to-load, with eye level view-finder.
- Handy attached black carrying strap.
- Uses standard No. 127 film, in black-and-white or full color.
- Synchronized for flash.

I—GROSS—8583—

These latest state of the art solid state DC Power Units are water cooled—have no fan or other moving parts. They are completely enclosed in NEMA 12 all welded (12 gauge steel) dust and oil proof cabinets. The cabinets are coated with blue epoxy and sealed with one coat of urethane.

Outstanding features of these units include: Complete AC and DC overload protection; Automatic controls; Solid state proportional voltage control; Remote control panel; Isolation transformers rated 125% of actual KVA requirement and totally epoxy impregnated.

Unit ratings available in current ranges from 250 to 10,000 amperes and up to 100 volts DC. Aging and deterioration are non-existant with their silicon controlled rectifiers and silicon full wave bridge power rectifiers.

(No added charge):
Automatic Current Density (ACD) or
Automatic Voltage Stabilized (AVS) er
Automatic Current Control (ACC).
(Additional charge):

Programmed Time Systems
Slope control for AVS or ACC (Quotations upon request).
Also available at an additional charge — Combinations of any of the standard controls and slope control and/or programmed systems (Quotations upon request).

Remote Control Panel with Meters

H.B.S. Solid State DC Power Supplies superior quality and operating benefits are as follows:

EFFICIENCY and RELIABILITY
Regulating and output control circuitry:
The power regulation of the output voltage and current is performed by solid state silicon controlled rectifier.
The advantages of the "SCR" are as follows:
1. Unlimited life—aging and deterioration are non-existant with silicon controlled rectifiers.
2. Highest peak reverse voltage rating—all units for 440/480 VAC input are supplied with 1200V PIV SCR with transient ratings of 1440V P.P. 230/240V units utilize 800V PIV SCRs 960V transient voltage.
3. Complete protection of SCR's against voltage transients.
4. Higher efficiency than any regulating device with comparable control range.
5. High power factor at least 90%, at rated input to output.
6. Unequaled response time—full on to off or off to full on—less than 50 milliseconds.
7. Continuous control from 0 to 100%, voltage and/or current
8. More than adequate cooling is provided for a maximum water temperature rise of 10° C (18°F) above ambient with the required water flow rate. Maximum water temperature 140° F.

TYPICAL GALLEY PROOFS

---

53 It is always better to be safe than sorry. This especially holds true when it comes to checking jobs before printing. Once it is printed it's too late to make changes or correct errors. It's a simple and inexpensive matter to request a proof of a type form if the job is being run **letterpress**. These made-up forms can be easily proofed and checked for last-minute changes or possible errors.

54 When **offset** printing is being employed it's best to have checked the pasted up artwork especially for changes since variations on the negatives can be time-consuming and quite costly. However, it is advisable to get a "brownline" of the negative so that any last minute changes could still be made. (Note—the overall image of a brownline is usually lighter or weaker than the image you will see in the printed sheet. A brownline does not necessarily indicate the final quality of the printing but rather allows you to see a print of the negatives without pasteup edges or other marks that are disturbing to the eye on a pasteup.)

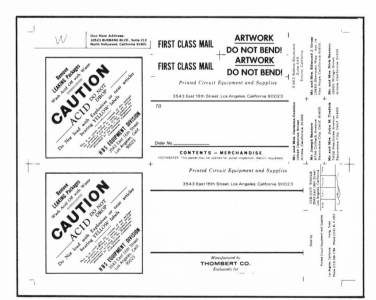

This brownline shows how several jobs are ganged up to save printing costs.

55 If you have pasted up type proofs on a dummy layout, don't make corrections or alterations on the proofs. Instead take the extra set of proofs the printer provides and make the necessary notations on them. It will save time and keep the dummy layout intact. It will also eliminate the need for the printer to check both the proofs and the dummy layout to compare corrections.

56 For only a few dollars you can have "Color Key" proofs of two, three or full-color jobs prior to printing. Seeing what the final job will look like before the plates are made can save considerable time, money and headaches later. These color proofs are made from the printer's negatives and are made for each of the colors that will appear on the job. There is some color limitation, however. The primary colors for 4-color (full-color) process work (yellow, red, blue and black) and a few other colors, including white, are available. There are enough colors, however, to allow you to see the finished job prior to printing. Consult your printer about Color Key before you give him your next job.

57 It's especially important when checking brownline proofs to check for broken letters, nicked periods, commas and hyphens. Opaquers have been known to paint out such letters. Also check all letters, rules, lines and borders. It's too late after the plate is made and the job is on the press. Printing jobs over because of nicked or damaged letters can be very costly.

Proofreader's Marks Most Commonly Used

∧	Make correction indicated in margin.
Stet	Retain crossed-out word or letter; let it stand.
.... Stet	Retain words under which dots appear; write "Stet" in margin.
×	Appears battered; examine.
≡	Straighten lines.
√√√	Unevenly spaced; correct spacing.
//	Line up; i.e., make lines even with other matter.
run in	Make no break in the reading; no ¶
no ¶	No paragraph; sometimes written "run in."
out see copy	Here is an omission; see copy.
¶	Make a paragraph here.
tr	Transpose words or letters as indicated.
♂ (dele)	Take out matter indicated; dele.
dele, close up	Take out character indicated and close up.
¢	Line drawn through a cap means lower case.
9	Upside down; reverse.
⁀‿	Close up; no space.
#	Insert a space here.
⊥	Push down this space.
□	Indent line one em.
[	Move this to the left.
]	Move this to the right.

⌐¬	Raise to proper position.
└┘	Lower to proper position.
////	Hair space letters.
w.f.	Wrong font; change to proper font.
Qu?	Is this right?
l.c.	Put in lower case (small letters).
s.c.	Put in small capitals.
Caps	Put in capitals.
C&S.C.	Put in caps and small caps.
rom.	Change to Roman.
ital.	Change to Italic.
≡	Under letter or word means caps.
=	Under letter or word, small caps.
—	Under letter or word means Italic.
~~	Under letter or word, bold face.
,/	Insert comma.
;/	Insert semicolon.
:/	Insert colon.
⊙	Insert period.
/?/	Insert interrogation mark.
(!)	Insert exclamation mark.
/=/	Insert hyphen.
∨'	Insert apostrophe.
∨" ∨"	Insert quotation marks.
e∨	Insert superior letter or figure.
∧1	Insert inferior letter or figure
[/]	Insert brackets.
(/)	Insert parenthesis.
1/m	One-em dash.
2/m	Two-em parallel dash.

CHAPTER 11

An Understanding of Paper Grades, Weights, Sizes, Colors and Finishes

Paper is made of two chief ingredients—wood pulp and rags. Some paper is made exclusively of wood, some is a combination of wood pulp and rags, while a few types are made from rags only.

By adding rag content to the manufacture of paper, it is strengthened, beautified and given longer life. Of course, the more rag content in a paper stock, the greater is the price.

The cheapest and shortest-lasting paper is newsprint. It fades very rapidly and is made to serve a specific purpose—to present a message that will not have to endure time.

Book papers are bleached and treated with sizing to harden their surface, thus lengthening their life span. There are many variations in book finishes. They range from antique to super-coated stock such as chrome coats. Coated paper was unknown prior to the invention of the halftone around 1880. But the halftone, to be reproduced faithfully, required smooth and hardened surfaces. Thus coated stock was developed since printing was mostly done by letterpress.

Now, with the advent of offset printing, stock surface is not too important to halftone printing since the image is transferred from plate to rubber blanket to paper—not direct from plate to paper as in letterpress. The rubber blanket tends to cushion the image onto the paper when transfer is made.

Keep in mind that when printing by letterpress where halftones are being used the paper grade is the determining factor for the halftone screen. One of the helpful hints in this chapter shows the proper halftone screen to use for a given paper stock. This puts limitations on your printing.

Offset printing, on the other hand, seems to defy most limitations. About the only thing coated stocks do for halftones is add lustre to the finished printed photo and add cost to the job because coated stock is more expensive. It also requires care in printing because varnishes and driers must be added to inks to prevent offset from the weight of previously printed sheets as they come off the press. It usually takes longer to produce a color job on coated stock than on other finishes because of drying time.

PAPER

This huge modern paper making machine is similar to the model used to produce the paper in this book. Photo courtesy of The Northwest Paper Co., Cloquet, MN.

Paper is divided into several grades—Book, Bond, Mimeo and Writing, Bristol and Board, Cover, Label, News, Thin and Carbonless. Each of these groups are further broken down·as follows:

BOOK—Coated and Uncoated.

BOND, MIMEO AND WRITING—Sulphite and Rag Bond, Ledger and Safety Paper, Mimeograph (Also included are envelopes made of bond paper).

BRISTOL AND BOARD—Index, Postcard, Plate and Vellum Card, Chrome Coat Card, Tag, Blanks, Placard, Boxboard, Railroad Board, Blotting, Pressboard and Chipboard.

COVER PAPER—Antique, Coated and Reversible (different color on each side).

LABEL—Regular Gummed, Dry Gummed and Pressure Sensitive.

NEWS—White Newsprint and Poster in white and colors.

THIN—Manifold, Bond, Parchment and Onionskin.

CARBONLESS—NCR type and 3M's Type 200. (Copies are made from these chemically treated papers without the need of carbon paper.)

Paper Weights. Each of the above mentioned grades of paper have a basic weight—i.e., the weight of 500 sheets of a standard mill size sheet. An example is 500 sheets of 17x22" bond weighs 16 lbs.

Here are some of the most common basic weights of stock by grades:

Bond, Mimeo and Writing Papers come in 13 lb., 16 lb., 20 lb. and 24 lb.

Bristol and Board stocks are 90 lb., 110 lb., 125 lb., 140 lb. and 3, 4, 5, 6, 8 and 10 ply.

Cover Paper—50 lb., 65 lb., 80 lb. and 130 lb. (double thick 65 lb.)

Label—50 lb. and 60 lb.

News comes in 32 lb.

Thin Papers are 8 lb., 9 lb. and 11 lb.

Carbonless varies—14 1/2 lb., 15 lb. and 20 lb.—due to chemicals on one or both sides.

The many **grades of paper** come in a wide selection of **sizes** for their **various weights**. The most common by category are:

Book Paper—17-1/2x22-1/2", 19x25", 23x29", 23x35" and 25x38". Most of these are also available in double sizes shown.

Bonds—17x22, 17x28 and 19x24". Also available in double sizes shown.

Bristol—17-1/2x22-1/2", 22x28", 22-1/2x28-1/2", 25-1/3x30-1/2", 22-1/2x 35" and 24x36".

Cover—20x26", 23x35" and 26x40".

Label—17x22" and 20x25".

News—24x36".

Thin Papers—17x22" and 17x28".

Carbonless—22-1/2x34-1/2" and 28-1/2x34-1/2".

Many of the above stocks are available in cut sizes such as 8-1/2x11" for bond stock and are ream wrapped (500 sheets to the package).

Printers know the sizes of all the various grades of paper and how best to cut them up with the least amount of waste allowing for bleeds and trimming on booklets and catalogs. Always check with your printer prior to planning a printed piece.

Paper comes in a **myraid of colors,** too. However, each grade has its own color characterists. For example: Bonds and mimeo usually are limited to white, canary, pink, blue, green and goldenrod. Some mills make salmon and green tint as standard colors. A few have other colors such as cafe (coffee color), ivory, india, grey and russett. Ask to see your printer's paper swatch books— you'll be amazed at the color variations even within a grade of paper such as bond or mimeo.

Besides the many colors available, paper comes in **numerous finishes**— pebble, linen, wove, antique, stipple, handmade, felt, mottled, suede, matte and many others.

The selection of the right paper for a printed job should be based on these points:

1. Choose a paper of appearance, weight and quality to fit the character of your message and your audience.

2. Keep the quality and price of paper in line with the price and quality of your product.

3. Buy the proper paper to suit the printing requirements—especially if letterpress is used.

4. Order a paper that is tough enough to hold up in the mails and for its intended use such as in a booklet or catalog.

5. Watch weights for postage—too heavy a sheet can tip the scales to the next ounce.

6. Use Cover Paper or Tagboard to protect booklets and catalogs—these papers are noted for their strength.

7. Don't overlook the importance of envelopes when ordering printing. It is the first thing seen by your prospects and customers.

STANDARD SIZES FOR VARIOUS PRINTED ITEMS MOST COMMONLY USED:

Business Cards — 2x3-1/2", 3-1/2x4" (Folder type)

Letterheads — 8-1/2x11", 7-1/4x10-1/2", 6x9" and 5-1/2x8-1/2"

Envelopes — **No. 10**—4-1/8x9-1/2", **No. 9**—3-7/8x8-7/8", **No. 8**—3-7/8x7-1/2", **No. 6-3/4**—3-5/8x6-1/2" and **No. 6-1/4**—3-1/2x6"

Catalog and Booklet Envelopes — 6x9", 7x10", 8-3/4x11-1/4", 9x12", 9-1/2x 12-1/2" and 10x13"

Shipping Labels — 3x5" and 4x5"

Invoices — 7x8-1/2" and 8-1/2x11"

Statements — 5-1/2x8-1/2" and 7x8-1/2"

Envelope Stuffers — 3-1/2x6-1/4" for 6-3/4 Envelopes.

Folders (page size) — 3-1/2x6-1/4", 4x9", 5-1/2x8-1/2", 6x9", 8-1/2x11" and 9x12"

Catalog Sheets — 8-1/2x11" and 11x17" (4 page)

Forms — 7x8-1/2", 8-1/2x11" and 8-1/2x14"

Broadsides — 17x22", 19x25", 20x26" and 23x35"

The above suggestions and the ones on the following pages can save you many dollars and headaches.

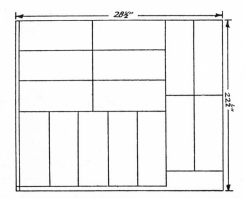

CUTTING 15 PIECES OF SIZE 4"X10" OUT OF A SHEET, SIZE 22½"X 28½"

HOW TO FIGURE

$$\frac{22\frac{1}{2} \times 28\frac{1}{2}}{10 \times 4}$$
$$2 \times \frac{2}{8} = \qquad 4$$

$$\frac{20\frac{1}{2} \times 22\frac{1}{2}}{10 \times 4}$$
$$2 \times \frac{3}{12} = \qquad 6$$

$$\frac{10\frac{1}{2} \times 20\frac{1}{2}}{10 \times 4}$$
$$1 \times 5 = \underline{\quad 5\quad}$$
$$15 \ PCS.$$

58 One of the surest ways to save money on all your printing is to use standard size paper for all your jobs. Always check sizes with your printer before you plan your job. Each type of paper has its own sizes as noted in the introduction to this chapter. Planning your job to use a size that cuts out of these standard sizes with a minimum of waste is advantageous. For example: 8 1/2x11" is a perfect size for Bond, Mimeo and Ledger. It is also the most common size for office use and filing. Even printing presses are designed to accomodate this standard size.

59 Watch the weight of the stock you will be using for that printed piece. Have a dummy from the actual stock made up by the printer and check it out for mailing weight. Remember when mailing first class that the next ounce of postage can cost you an extra stamp or double your mailing cost. There are many good papers that have the opacity you need, yet, are lightweight.

60 More and more jobs today are being printed by offset. However, if you are using letterpress, be sure to check the printing surface of the paper before you order any halftones (photo engravings). This formula can save you a lot of headaches and money: **The finer the screen you use on the engraving, the finer the stock must be.** Rough stocks will not take fine engravings—screens must be coarse. Here is a list of proper engraving screens for various stocks:

    65 lines—Newsprint and other rough stocks.
    85 lines—Cheaper bonds, finer newsprint, smooth book.
    100 lines—Machine finish papers, supercoated and bonds.
    120 lines—Magazine, book stock, dull coated stocks, high grade bonds.
    133 lines—Most commonly used for high coated book stock or chrome
           finish stock.

61   On jobs requiring folding on heavy stocks such as cover paper and cardboard always be certain the **grain** is the right way for folding (it should be the same as the fold if possible). For example, if the job is run on 9x12" stock and folded in thirds to approximately 4x9" then the grain should be the 9" way. The reason for this is that if the grain is not with the fold you'll find yourself paying for an extra bindery or press operation—the cost of scoring the stock before folding.

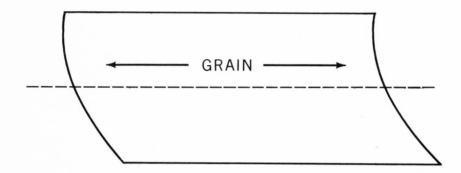

GRAIN

62   If you have documents or other valuable papers to be printed that must last for many years then have them printed on rag content paper. The more rag content in the paper, the longer the form will last. Rag content is available in bond, ledger and index stocks and can vary from 25% to 100%—prices increasing with the greater percent of rags used. Not only does rag content paper last longer, it also wears better if needed for constant use. Currency is printed from the best grades of rag paper available for it must take constant use and abuse for long periods of time. There are some limitations in the printing on rag papers. The greatest one being that fine screen halftones reproduce better by offset than by letterpress. This is no real problem since more and more printing is being done by offset today.

CHAPTER 12

Shortcuts for Ordering Negatives, Plates and Engravings

In each process of printing—Letterpress and Offset—there is need for plates of one form or another to carry the printed image.

In **letterpress** a plate is not always necessary. Many jobs can be printed from type, ornaments, rules and borders. But where illustrations and photographs are required along with the type, plates are essential. The plates used in letterpress printing are called **engravings.** Other names are given them such as **zincs** or **cuts**—with cuts being the most commonly used.

Engravings are spaced and locked up with type forms to be printed together. Type ornaments, rules and borders can also be combined with illustrations or photos to make up a single engraving such as is used in ads. This type of work should be prepared by a commercial art service or an advertising agency to be sure it's done correctly. However, it is not always advisable to make a combination engraving if there are going to be future changes. It's better to keep type separate from illustrations and photos for more flexibility and lower costs.

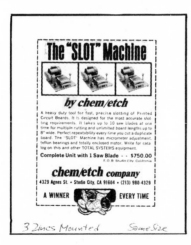
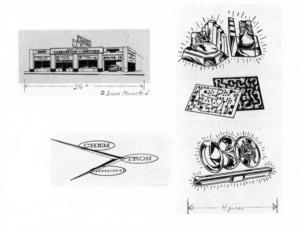

Several pieces of copy are shown here to illustrate the variety of work an engraver does — line art, ads and photographs.

Before you can order an engraving you need camera-ready artwork or copy. The engraver must have some form of copy from which to make your engraving. This includes type repro proofs, artwork or photographs.

Once he has your copy, he places it in the copy board of his camera and makes the necessary adjustments for the required finished size negative. For best results have copy shot same size or reduced if at all possible.

The negative which the engraver makes from your copy is now trimmed for excess area and placed with others to form a "flat" of negatives directly on the zinc (or magnesium) to be engraved.

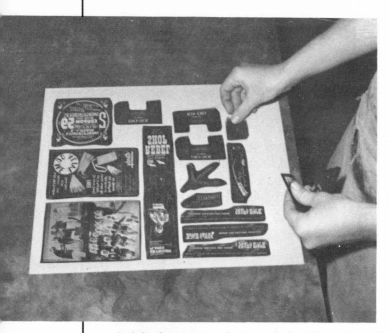

At left, the engraver is seen placing trimmed negatives onto a sensitized zinc plate. This assembly is called a "flat." At right, the plate is being exposed to arc light for several minutes in a vacuum frame. Photo taken at Publishers Engraving Co., North Hollywood, CA.

This metal (about 1/16" thick) is next placed in a glass top vacuum frame. Securely locked in the vacuum frame the plate is exposed to an arc light which burns the negative images onto its sensitized surface. After several minutes of exposure to the arc light, the negatives are removed from the plate.

The plate is now developed so the engraver can see the image. It is next treated with special compound which covers the image. The purpose of the compound is to prevent acid from eating the image during the actual engraving process. After careful treating of the plate, it is placed in an acid bath where the parts that are not to print are eaten away by the acid. The plate is removed several times and checked for depth of etching. It is treated again and again with more protective compound until it is etched to the required depth. If the etched (non-printing) areas are too shallow, the engraver will have too much hand tooling to do since the low areas must be low enough so as not to receive ink from the printer's letterpress.

Above, engraver is touching up nicked letters, pinholes and other imperfections on the exposed and developed plate. At left, he is removing the finished engraved plate.

After the large zinc plate is correctly acid etched it is routed—all areas that are not to print must be safely low. After routing all the individual jobs on the plate are cut apart and mounted on special hardwood to make them **type high**—.918 inch. (All printer's type, rules, borders, etc., are this height.)

Engraving is a slow and costly process. For engravers to make money they must gang their jobs to keep production costs at a minimum. There are many ways to save money on your engravings which you will find in this chapter.

Mounted "cuts."

Routing excess metal from around individual engravings and cutting shallow non-printing areas deeper.

Plates for **offset** printing are entirely different than letterpress plates (engravings). First of all the process of printing is not the same—letterpress being printed from a raised or bas relief surface, while offset is printed from a flat (even or planographic) surface. Letterpress printing uses ink on its raised surface while the offset process inks and water dampens a thin metal plate whose flat surface is slightly grained. The principle is that water and grease (ink) do not mix. Ink adheres only to the image being repelled from blank areas by the water. Letterpress is printed directly onto the paper—offset is first printed onto a rubber blanket, then this image is transferred to the paper.

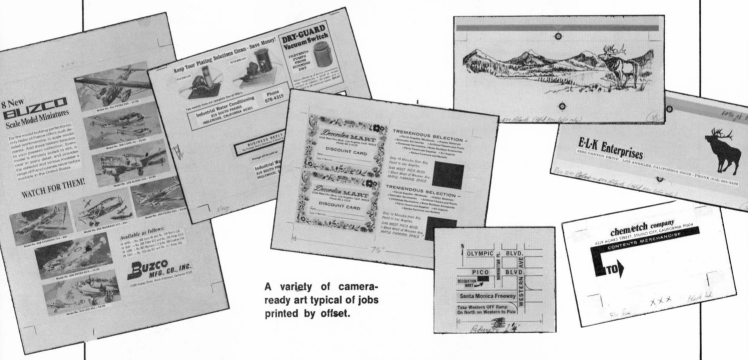

A variety of camera-ready art typical of jobs printed by offset.

Plate making for offset printing requires good camera-ready copy. If copy is camera-ready it is already made up in its finished form—type, artwork and photos are all in place on one piece of artboard. (See Chapter 9 on Pasteup). This copy is shot the same as copy shot for engravings— i.e., a negative is made of it. The negative, or negatives, if several pages are to be run at the same time on a large press, are stripped up (assembled) onto a sheet of orange opaque paper. The image areas that are to print are opened up with a razor blade. The negatives are then opaqued for pin holes and other unwanted marks that might print. At this point a brownline print can be made of the assembled **flat** which allows you a final look at the job before it is plated.

To the left is an offset "flat" which is a negative of camera-ready art stripped onto a piece of opaque paper. To the right the printer is preparing a "flat" and plate for exposure.

To make an offset plate the negative flat is placed over a sensitized piece of aluminum about .010" thick. The plate must be flexible so it can be wrapped around a press cylinder. The negative and plate are locked in a glass top vacuum frame. An arc light is used to expose the open areas (image) of the negative onto the plate. After exposure or **burning** the negative is removed and the plate is developed up with chemical dye, washed and gummed to protect its surface. It is now ready for the press.

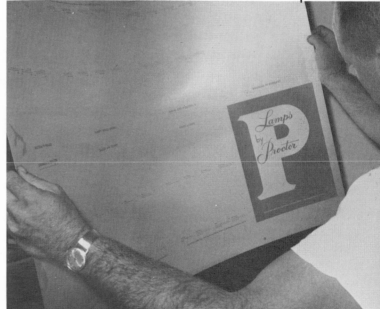

Photos taken at Rapid Graphics, North Hollywood, CA

Developing an offset plate (left) so the image is visible. The developed plate is seen in the picture at the right. It is now ready for the offset press.

Making an offset plate is a much simpler and faster process than making a letterpress engraving. Actually the principle is little more than that used in photography—making a print off a negative, only instead of paper, a metal plate is used.

This chapter contains several valuable pointers for ordering engravings and offset negatives and plates. However, always keep in mind that good clean camera-ready copy can save you the most money in this department of printing. Your engravings and offset plates can only be as good as the copy you furnish.

The following is what is considered as "good" camera copy:
1. Black and white line copy of type preferably in repro form.
2. Original black and white artwork—line, wash or opaque.
3. Velox prints of photos, wash drawings and opaque artwork.
4. Previously printed matter on clean white stock (line and halftones with coarse screens—not over 110 line). Copy on enamel stock picks up best.
5. Previously printed matter on light colored stocks (cream, ivory, off-white, canary or light blue). These must be printed in black ink. Not usually recommended to be pasted down with good clean black and white copy. It is best to have photostats made of this copy first and then paste down the stats with the black and white copy. If there is not time to have stats made of these colored stocks, they can be shot separately and stripped into the black and white negatives by the engraver or printer.

The following types of copy should **never** be included along with good black and white copy:
1. Newsprint clippings. These should be shot separately and made into black and white photostats and pasted down with other black and white copy or shot separately and stripped into negatives by the printer or engraver.
2. Strong colored papers with colored inks on them. These have to be shot with special color filters on the camera to eliminate background colors and bring out the printing color desired.
3. Yellow and blue ink copy printed on the same sheet. These colors cannot be filtered out together. Each color must be filtered out separately thus increasing your negative cost.

If you must use filtered color copy have black and white prints made from the negs shot and paste these prints down with other black and white art on an artboard as camera-ready copy.

For the best possible work always use black and white copy whenever possible. Filtered copy generally shows some variation from the original.

TYPES OF HALFTONES AVAILABLE SHOWING MAGNIFIED DOT STRUCTURE

SQUARE HALFTONE
(100 Lines)

HIGHLIGHT HALFTONE
(100 Lines)

OUTLINE HALFTONE
(100 Lines)

VIGNETTE HALFTONE
(100 Lines)

A highly magnified portion of halftone showing dot structure.

63   If a halftone is to be used in a publication, the screen should always be the one specified in the publication rate card. Check with the newspaper or magazine or their representative and get their latest rate card.

64   If you are ordering a number of engravings to be made in the same reduction, group the artwork or photos on one mounting board, allowing space for sawing apart (at least 1/4" between items), and save the cost of separate engravings. The engraver will charge you for the maximum size engraving plus a small cutting charge for each individual piece of art or photo on the group. Many dollars can be saved with this method of **ganging** your engravings. Sometimes it even pays to start accumulating your art and photos to make up a gang shot. Remember to keep line artwork and photos separate unless the photos have been veloxed and will shoot as line artwork (see Chapter 8, Photostats, Negatives and Prints).

This paste-up contains a variety of trademarks, slogans, address lines and other regularly used items for present and future printing pieces.

65   Should you expect to reorder any engraving from copy now in the engraver's shop, ask him to hold your negatives. This could save you the cost of making new negatives. Engravers do not generally provide negatives to customers, since what you are buying is the finished engraving. They usually destroy the negatives after a reasonable time.

66 Whenever you can order your offset negatives to be billed separately from your printing. By owning your negatives you can use them in many ways without having to pay for them over and over. For example—if you need trademarks, signatures, artwork and photos (halftones) that are incorporated on one negative, you can have a print made from the neg (in whole or in part) and use portions of the print for several different jobs. You can save many dollars by owning your own negs. On reruns with or without changes you'll find it's very convenient to have your own negs especially if your printer is too busy to print your job in an emergency. Being able to take the negatives to another printer is always a convenience.

67 When ordering engravings try to keep them simple by furnishing the camera-ready artwork in one piece if at all possible to do so. For example, if you have type matter, handlettered words or headlines, artwork or other elements to be combined on a single engraving, mount them on one artboard. If handlettering and art are too big or too small you can have photostats made to size. The correct sizes can be rubber cemented along with your type repro proofs to one artboard. This will enable the engraver to make one shot of your job at a fixed price. If he has to shoot and strip up separate negatives of each of these elements you'll pay quite a bit more. This type of composite engraving is called a **combination** engraving and can be very costly because it is time-consuming for the engraver. You can do the pasteup for little or no money yourself with just a few basic tools—a small artboard (breadboard type), T-Square, Angle (30-60° and/or 45°), rubber cement and brush, X-Acto knife and rubber cement pickup eraser. See chapter 9 on Pasteup. Most engravers would rather receive work that is camera-ready.

68 The best way to mark art for reduction or enlargement is as follows:

Specifications

Reduce 19½ picas to 13 picas

Measure the art in printers' picas rather than in inches and fractions of inches. Then mark **REDUCE** ___picas to ___picas, or **ENLARGE** ___picas to ___ picas. If the final measure is critical, note this with **MUST BE EXACT.**

Above is a single color pasteup. Below are duplicate negatives of the above pasteup. The negative on the left has been opaqued for color, while the one on the right is for black.

69   Always have complicated pasteup artwork color separated where two or more colors are to be printed. If you depend upon the printer or engraver to separate the colors for you, your cost will be considerably higher than having it done on the artwork. However, simple artwork where only headlines and special words are to be in a second color can be inexpensively done by camera. The printer or engraver shoots two negatives of the black and white pasteup and paints out the unwanted color on each negative. By placing register marks ✛ on the copy before he shoots he is able to match up the negatives after they have been painted out and thus will have separated color negatives for both black and color plates. You should furnish a tissue overlay to show what items are to be printed in the second color.

70   Do not use an enormous size piece of artboard to pasteup an ad or brochure that is of small size. This habit is commonly practiced by large advertising agencies to impress their big spending clients and does nothing to enhance the art as far as the printer or engraver is concerned. It's not only costly for artboard but is difficult for the cameraman to handle especially if same size or enlarged negatives are needed. Here is how artwork should and should not be positioned on artboard:

Less expensive and more practical way to prepare art or copy for engraver or printer.

Wasteful method of doing artwork or pasteup.

71   The normal procedure in buying offset printing is for the printer to furnish you the number of finished printed copies and retain rights over the negatives and plates. They are his property since he only contracted to do a printing job from your layout or artwork. To help you keep the costs of reprinting down, it is wise to ask your printer if you may purchase the negatives separately. Some will and others won't sell them to you as a separate item. Another way to have the negatives in your possession for future use is to have them made by a lithographic negative and plate service. Many printers use these services when they do not have a camera of their own or when their own facilities are overloaded. The posession of plates is not too important since they deteriorate and do not always fit another printer's press. But negatives are important.

72   When ordering veloxes of photos be sure to specify if they are to be used for letterpress (engravings) or for offset printing. The reason for this is that when they are shot as halftones for letterpress reproduction the finished printing seems to become contrasty. In offset printing the opposite is true—they become flatter looking and lose their sharp look. Therefore, the cameraman shoots the letterpress veloxes with less contrast (more middle or gray tones) and the veloxes for offset with more contrast (less middle or gray tones). You will be less disappointed with the results if you remember the above in ordering veloxes.

CHAPTER 13

Printing—How to Get More For Your Money

Two printing processes—letterpress and offset—are the most commonly used for everyday printing needs. This entire book contains time- and money-saving ideas for these two methods of reproduction.

Since the advent of offset printing many printers today print only by offset, others by offset and letterpress, with some still using only letterpress.

Figures for 1969 on printing done by various processes are as follows:

	1969
Letterpress	39%
Offset	52%
Gravure and Silk Screen	9%

Tremendous inroads have been made by offset over the past 20 years. However, letterpress is still holding its own and will continue to do so for many years. It is still the quickest method known to run a job direct from type setups, especially short runs or small size jobs such as business cards, post cards, announcements, tickets, tags and imprinting on previously printed pieces. Printing direct from type eliminates the added expense of negatives and plates as in offset.

Here is a brief description of the principle of the two most popular printing processes.

Letterpress—Printing from type is known as **relief** printing. The image that is to print is raised higher than the surrounding area. Ink is then applied to this image. The inked surface is brought in contact with paper and is pressed against the paper to make an impression. The image is then reinked and im-

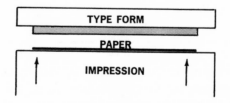

pressed against a new sheet of paper and so on. Letterpress can be printed on three types of presses—platen, cylinder and rotary.

Most job printers have platen type presses. Paper is fed into them by hand or automatically. Some job printers have cylinder presses as well as platen presses. The cylinder press can do a better job since printing is done only on that part of the cylinder which is impressing the paper against the inked type

PRINTING

Platen type letterpress with automatic Kluge feeder.

form as it is turning. This tangent impression gives a smooth, uniform printed image and can be much better controlled than platen type printing which smashes into the type form in one overall impression. Cylinder press printing is also a faster process providing more impressions per hour.

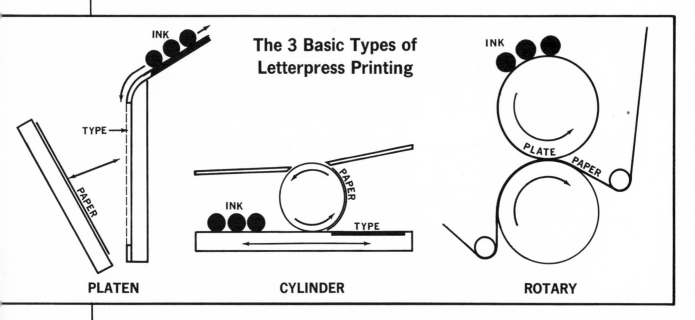

The 3 Basic Types of Letterpress Printing

INK

TYPE

PAPER

PLATEN

INK

PAPER

TYPE

CYLINDER

INK

PLATE

PAPER

ROTARY

Printing by rotary offers the advantage of high speed and is best suited for long press runs of hundreds of thousands or more copies. The rotary principle is similar to the cylinder method except the image form is made into a curved plate which fits around a cylinder. This inked plate is pressed onto paper fed from a continuous roll against an impression cylinder. Some of the most beautiful printing in the world is done by this method. Most of the large general magazine publications still use rotary letterpress—Better Homes and Gardens, Life, Ladies Home Journal and many others. Most daily newspapers are still printed by rotary letterpress using stereotype metal plates.

Photo taken at Macson Printing & Lithography, Glendale, CA.

Pressman is locking plate onto offset press cylinder.

Offset printing is entirely different than letterpress. Instead of printing direct from a typeset form, a proof must first be made of the type form and them a camera shot made of the proof. The resulting negative is then exposed onto a sensitized thin metal plate. This plate is developed and wrapped around a cylinder on an offset press which has an inking system and a chemical/water dampening system. When the plate rotates it is dampened by the chemical/water system. As it passes beneath the ink rollers only the image receives ink— the non-image areas repell the ink because of the dampness. The process is based on the principle that water and grease (ink) do not mix.

After being properly inked, the image is transferred to a rubber blanket on another cylinder. Next a sheet of paper passes through the press between the rubber blanket cylinder and an impression cylinder to receive the image from the rubber blanket. The image has been "offset" from the blanket onto the sheet of paper rather than printed directly onto the sheet as in letterpress.

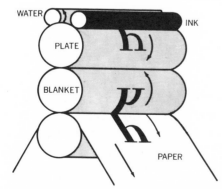

Above illustrates the offset printing process. Pressman in photo at right is making final adjustments prior to printing on this 23x29" press.

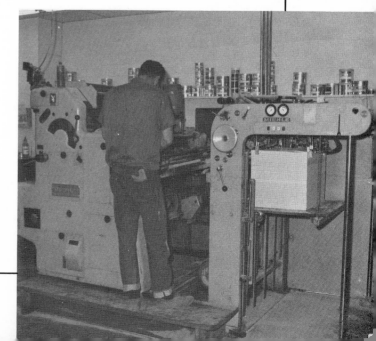

The entire process is properly called **offset** lithography or planographic printing since no image appears raised in relief on the metal plate.

Printing by offset is rapidly becoming the most popular method of reproducing literature of all types. It has been simplified so that office help can now operate offset duplicator machines with little or no effort and minimal training. For black and white jobs or simple color work, the offset duplicator is ideal. However, not every office needs one or can afford the investment of several thousand dollars for the limited work they may require.

Because of the need for quick-print forms, data sheets and price lists, the instant offset print shop was created. These shops specialize in 8-1/2x 11" or 8-1/2x14" size forms in black ink at a very reasonable price. Copy must be camera-ready and be clean and sharp for best results. Not every city or town has this type of printer. At the moment they seem to be most popular in the larger cities.

Top quality offset printing of large size color jobs requires the skill and equipment only qualified print shops offer. Always inquire about a printer's equipment before giving him your work. Ask to see similar work he has done for others. Too many jobs are run on incorrect size presses and results are usually less than desired by the buyer. Offset printing offers you a very flexible means of getting good quality work reasonably if you take the time to look for the right printer. This same care should apply to letterpress printed jobs.

73   Repeat your best printed advertising pieces more frequently and save in several ways. (1) You will not have to pay for new artwork as often, (2) You can order larger quantities of the printed matter that pulls the best and get a better price break for printing, (3) You can change the color of ink or stock or both and make the same printing piece look like new again.

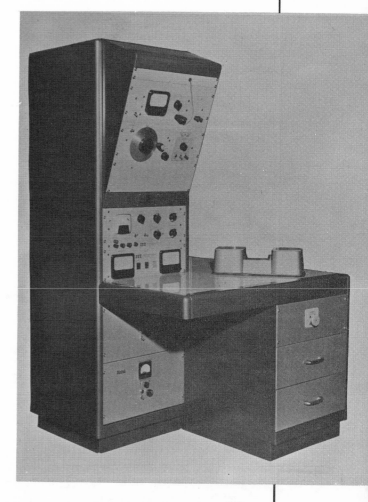

Examples of a "non-bleed" (above) and "bleed" (right). Allowance must be made for oversize paper as well as trim area on photos and artwork on "bleed" jobs.

74   Bleed jobs which print to the edges of the paper can be more costly especially if run on small presses where paper has to be purchased oversize and trimmed after printing. Also, ink coverage generally is not as good as when jobs are run on larger presses with adequate inking rollers.

75   Getting more use from color engravings or color separated negatives can save a good deal of money. Proofs of the color separations (yellow, red, blue and black) can be blown up with a camera to two or more times their normal size and be used for poster, point of purchase displays and window streamers. Each color plate must be proofed in black ink and noted as to its real color. The dots will increase accordingly — 120 line screen will enlarge to a 60 line screen if blown up twice size, to 40 lines if enlarged three times its original size, etc. However, from a distance, no one will see the difference in the coarser screen. If you do not have engravings but instead have color separated negatives from offset printing, then you can make prints of each of the color negatives (again identifying them by their proper colors) and have the prints blown up the same as you would the engraved color proofs. By this method of utilizing your color negs and plates you will have saved many dollars by not having to pay for new color separations. And those large size separations can be quite costly—$200 or more for just a set of color negatives.

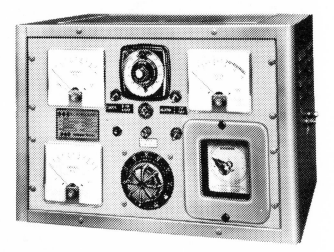

A 110 line velox is shown above. To the right is the same velox blown up twice size with the screen being correspondingly enlarged to 55 line. By looking at this page from a distance the coarser dots do not stand out.

76   When you use 4-color printing and require several color photographs to be included on a page or in a catalog consider having duplicate photos made to their finished sizes. Then trim and paste (with rubber cement) the finished photos to your artboard for one separation (4 camera shots—1 each for yellow, red, blue and black). The final color separation which is very costly if several photos must be color separated individually can then be made in a single separation. Here's a comparative example of what a color job of one page having five color photos would cost if done by each method:

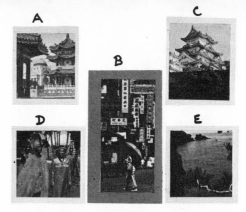

GET TRAVEL ORIENTED

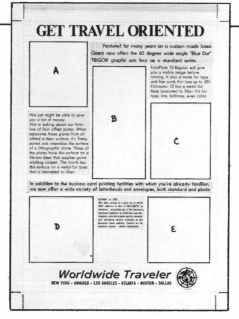

PASTEUP METHOD

Color Copies (Photographic Prints
   made by your photographer)
   5 at $3.00 each $15.00

Color Separation from Pasteup of
   the 5 above photo prints
   (Approx. final neg size
   10x12") 85.00
                  Total—$100.00

STRIP-IN METHOD

Color Separation of all
   5 Prints if shot individually
   to sizes indicated on pasteup.

5 (Approx. 4x5") Negs
   at $45.00 each $225.00

Savings **$125.00**

You save about $125.00 by using the Pasteup Method over the Strip-In Method. The above figures do not include color correction or retouching. You should consult your printer about this beforehand. There is some extra charge if color correction or retouching is necessary. But it usually will be more than offset by the above savings if the photography has been professionally done.

(Note—the above prices are based on average figures for color separation and do not necessarily mean they are the same in every locality. You should check with your printer for his prices to make your own comparisons.)

77 It costs you nothing extra for printing to add a headline or a block of copy to an envelope you are running anyway. This added attention-getter can do much to get the readers' attention.

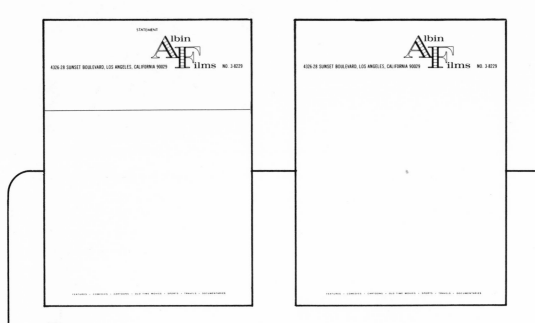

78 Where only a small quantity of invoices or statements are needed, have them printed with your letterheads as shown here.

Have the printer set the letterhead and add the word **INVOICE** or **STATEMENT** to the top of the sheet. If a line is desired to separate the letterhead and address areas from the billing section he can add this too, as well as a dot to guide you in addressing. If he is printing by letterpress, he need only stop the press, take the type form out of the press and substitute blank spaces for the word **INVOICE** or **STATEMENT** and the line and/or dot. After making these changes he puts the form back in the press and continues to print your letterheads.

If the job is printed by offset, the printer erases the words **INVOICE** or **STATEMENT** and the line and/or dot from the metal plate and proceeds to print the job as a letterhead. The charge for making the changes in either process is minimal.

The chief advantage of this method of getting invoices or statements and letterheads is the savings of not having to print the items as separate jobs.

Let us assume you require 500 to 800 letterheads yet only have use for 100 to 200 invoices or statements. The printer will charge the same to run 1000 sheets of paper with or without changes. There will usually be a slight charge for removing the word **INVOICE** or **STATEMENT** and the line and/or dot, but it's nothing compared to having 100 or 300 statements or invoices printed as a separate job. It is advisable to run extra statements or invoices even though you may never need them. Example—800 letterheads and 200 statements = a 1000 sheet press run. Other combinations in any various quantities can be worked out with your printer. Always buy in reams (500 sheets) or in 1000 sheet quantities since paper is ream wrapped. In many cases you'll be charged for the stock if you use it or not. And you certainly will pay for a minimum press charge of 1000 impressions if you run them or not.

The statements or invoices can be trimmed to a shorter length if the full size 8-1/2x11" sheet is not needed.

79 Here's how to get the effect of several color combinations when printing news bulletins, catalog sheets, house organs and data sheets without the costly color runs with each black run. Design a layout that can be used as a permanent part of the data sheet or bulletin. Print this design in a variety of colors on white or colored stock to get several colors ahead. For example, if you are going to mail 500 bulletins per month, then print 1000 of each of six different colors so you can alternate colors for the first six months and repeat these colors again in the following six months. The extra charge you get from the printer for washups and color inks will be minimal compared to putting the job on the press to run the color with the black each time you mail. You get the use of a single piece of artwork, the power of repetition and a savings in printing (larger press run) and stock (you can usually buy stock for less when you order at least 5000 sheets).

80 To print both sides of a job at one time on those two-sided jobs have your printer run it "work and turn" or "work and tumble." This means that instead of a job of 5000 pieces being run through a press twice (5000 impressions on each side), both sides will be run through on one side of the sheet, turned over and printed again on the opposite side (2500 impressions for each side). The paper is double its normal size to accomodate the two forms. Presswork is cut in half with this method of printing. Items which are perfect for "work and turn" or "work and tumble" jobs are folder type business cards, reply cards, mailer cards, envelope stuffers, prices lists and catalog sheets.

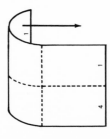

This is a "work and turn" job which when printed and cut apart will make two 4-page folders.

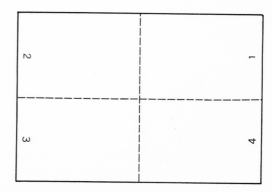

81 Get estimates in writing especially when jobs are complicated and involve large amounts of money. The best way to get an accurate estimate is to furnish complete specifications of the job to the printer. Here is a typical form which gives all the information you'll need for most printed jobs. It's always wise to have the printer give you estimates on various quantities. You may find that for a few dollars more you can get thousands of additional pieces and thus eliminate the need for a rerun at a later date. Of course this only pays if there are no changes anticipated in the future and you are definitely going to use the literature.

YOUR LETTERHEAD

REQUEST FOR PRINTING QUOTATION

To: Date:

1. Description of printed piece:

2. Size of piece:

3. Quantity to be printed:

4. Number of colors:

5. Finishing desired:

6. Imprinting (if any):

7. Copy will be supplied as follows:

8. Date estimate wanted:

9. Delivery date:

10. Method of delivery:

Requested by_____

82 **Watch those minimum charges**! Most everyone in the graphic arts industry has minimum basic charges for various functions of work. These minimums can run anywhere from $5.00 to $25.00 depending upon the shop. For example, a high quality type house may have a $15.00 minimum charge to set **one word** or **one paragraph** of copy in type. Or a printer may charge not less than $10.00 to do any print job if only 50 copies are needed. So it goes all down the line in the printing trade as well as in other trades.

There are ways to beat these fixed initial costs:

1. Plan your work well in advance of your needs.
2. Group several similar jobs together (one size and style of type.)
3. Don't make alterations and changes on work once it's set up or in negative form unless **absolutely necessary**.
4. Have sufficient copies run while on the press. There is only a very minimal cost to run greater amounts than required. On the other hand the cost to put the job back on the press for only 100 copies can be quite costly.

Here is a list of preparatory or makeready costs for various facets of the printing trade:

Typesetting—Charge is made for each type style, size and line length change on a linotype machine.

Charge is made for each makeup and repro proof.

Charge is made for each proofreading.

Presswork—Charge is made for lockup of type forms (letterpress only).

Charge is made for press makeready.

Charge is made for washups when color ink is used.

Charge is made for mixing special color inks (use standard colors whenever possible to do so).

Bindery—Charges for setups on folding machines, drills, stitchers, perforators, scorers, cutters and trimmers.

83 A duotone effect can be had for little or no cost by having the printer mix color ink into his black ink. Such colors as brown, red, blue or green, when added to the black being used on the run will not show as color on borders, type or other solid areas, but will show as a duotone effect on the halftones that are included with the run. This method is only feasible where halftones are used and can save the cost of a halftone duotone negative, stripping, extra plate and press run. The effect will not be too startling but will add a touch of color and give a pleasing color effect at minimal cost.

84   Getting the exact number of copies you order in printing may be very important to you for certain jobs. However, the printing trade custom only guarantees delivery to **10% over or under** your requirements. Therefore, be certain to specify "exact quantity" when ordering your next printing job, especially if it's a 2, 3 or 4-color job that requires costly makereadies and large quantities of paper spoilage. Reruns to make up shorted runs can be very costly.

85   Remember this—inks do not print the same on coated stocks as they do on uncoated stocks. Ask your printer to show you samples of ink colors on both types of stock and prevent disappointment with results. Better still, get yourself an ink sample book from an ink house.

86   The next time you have corner cards printed on envelopes have the printer run a few 110 pound index cards through his press while running your envelopes. A hundred or so of these cards might only amount to a couple of dollars or less and will give you a ready stock of postcards you can use for order acknowledgements, quick notes or other uses without the need of using your more expensive stationery. (Stock should be run same size as envelopes, then trimmed to size desired.)

87   Gang printing of small jobs can save you money and keep you supplied with printed matter. Typical items that can be advantageously ganged are— business cards, business reply cards, envelope stuffers, labels, memos and phone pads and small forms for everyday office use.

    Shown here is a group of items printed on cover stock that were ganged on a small press. Besides saving money on printing it gave uniformity to the theme of the event. For example, the two top items and the one on the lower right were used as mailers (the opposite side of the sheet being unprinted for addressing and stamps), the Invitation in the lower left corner was sent in an envelope, leaving the Admission Ticket in the center left. Note also that very little typesetting was done. Stock art was used along with speedball pen lettering and typewriter to get the special effects while keeping economy in mind. Many types of grouping such as this one can be made very economically. Figure the press run to include the largest quantity needed for a particular item. In some cases the most needed items can be ganged two or more times along with the other items. Whichever way you decide to gang run work you'll find it economical and fast.

"I SEE A DANCE IN YOUR FUTURE—A BIG AFFAIR—ONE YOU CANNOT AFFORD TO MISS! IT'S THE ANNUAL LOYOLA LAW SCHOOL DANCE, THIS YEAR AT THE LA BREAKFAST CLUB, 3201 LOS FELIZ BLVD. THIS DATE IS IMPORTANT: SATURDAY, FEBRUARY 20TH. I SEE MANY FRIENDS OF YOURS, SOME WITH AWARDS FOR *OUTSTANDING DEEDS*. I SEE AN ORCHESTRA, PRIZES, REFRESHMENTS. IT WILL BE THE FIRST TIME ALUMNI WILL ATTEND"

"CONFOUND IT! OF COURSE I'M GOING TO THE LOYOLA LAW SCHOOL DANCE ON SATURDAY, FEBRUARY 20TH. WOULDN'T MISS THIS BIG EVENT FOR THE WORLD, ESPECIALLY WHEN THEY'RE INVITING US ALUMNI FOR THE VERY FIRST TIME...WHERE? THE LA BREAKFAST CLUB, 3201 LOS FELIZ BLVD. IT'S ONLY $2 PER COUPLE, TOO! I HEAR THERE'LL BE A GOOD ORCHESTRA—NAME OF JOHNNY DELFINO... THAT'S RIGHT, EVERYBODY WILL BE THERE! I UNDERSTAND THAT AWARDS WILL BE GIVEN TO OUTSTANDING ALUMNI... SEE YOU THERE!"

STUDENT ADMISSION

Loyola Law School Dance
for Students and Alumni
LA Breakfast Club, 3201 Los Feliz Blvd.

SATURDAY, FEBRUARY 20, 1960
9:00 p.m. to 1:00 a.m.

Donation $2.00 per Couple
Dress Optional

Music by Johnny Delfino
and His Orchestra

Your Invitation to the
Loyola Law School Dance
for Students and Alumni
at the
LA Breakfast Club, 3201 Los Feliz Blvd.

SATURDAY, FEBRUARY 20, 1960
9:00 p.m. to 1:00 a.m.

Donation $2.00 per Couple
Dress Optional

Music by Johnny Delfino
and His Orchestra

ALUMNI BEING INVITED TO LOYOLA LAW SCHOOL DANCE FOR FIRST TIME

Loyola Law School Alumni will have the opportunity to meet old friends from their school days at the law school students annual dance on Saturday, February 20th at the LA Breakfast Club, 3201 Los Feliz Blvd. This is a first-time invitation to the alumni and a big turnout is anticipated.

AWARDS WILL BE PRESENTED

The dance committee is happy to announce that Special Awards will be given to outstanding alumni at this big affair.

Music will be by Johnny Delfino and his orchestra and there will be prizes and refreshments. Dress is optional. Bids of $2.00 per couple will be sent to all alumni in the very near future.

The Printing Specialist—When to Use His Services. Once you know your printing needs you'll be able to plan your reordering farther ahead and save considerable money by using the printing specialist. Certain printed items are produced by these specially equipped tradesmen at very low prices. In fact, there is no comparison to their prices and those of your local printer. Some of the items commonly produced by specialty houses are envelopes, business forms, labels and tags.

The newest member to the fold is the Instant Printing Shop where you can get from 100 to 1000 copies of black and white printing for less money than at any local printing job shop. Check your local yellow pages for companies which do specialty printing and compare prices. You'll see the difference of what a little planning and patience can make in dollars saved.

Here is a list of printing Specialists to help you in looking up local firms for your specific needs:

Balloons	Indexing and Tabbing
Banners	Labels
Book Covers	Maps
Book Matches	Menus
Boxes	Newspapers
Bumper Stickers	Packaging
Calendars	Pencils and Pens
Cellophane	Plastic
Decals	Posters and Billboards
Embossing	Ribbons and Buttons
Envelopes	Stationery
Forms	Tags
Full-Color Printing	Thermography (Raised printing)
Gummed Tape	Tickets

CHAPTER 14

Bindery Shortcuts

Before a printing job is started, careful thought must be given to bindery requirements if any are needed. Too many jobs are well into the printing stage before bindery is ever considered. Much trouble can be avoided if bindery planning is done in the layout stages of a printed piece.

Jobs that require folding, stitching and trimming, especially require careful planning. Allowances must be made for proper folding (right angle or parallel), if the job is to be side stitched, saddle stitched, perfect bound, plastic or spiral bound, and how much trim will be required to finish the job.

Always check with your printer and/or binder before proceeding with any job that requires bindery work. He'll help you plan out your job from your layout so your pasteup will be properly positioned if several pages are put on one piece of artboard. He'll tell you how much gutter space to leave, how much allowance you need for bleeds and other time- and money-saving production tips.

Six types of book bindings commonly used are shown here:

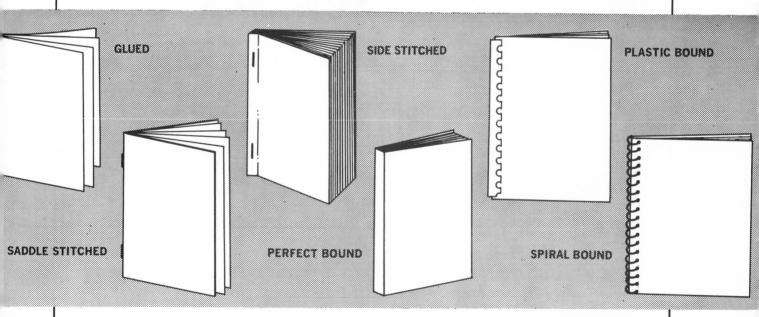

GLUED   SIDE STITCHED   PLASTIC BOUND

SADDLE STITCHED   PERFECT BOUND   SPIRAL BOUND

Often times an inexpensive advertising mailing piece can be **glued** while being folded. This method of binding is very popular with newspaper or sale catalog type mailers or giveaways of eight or more pages. For better quality work the type of binding depends upon the thickness of the booklet or book, its life expectancy, its particular use and how much your budget can stand.

BINDERY

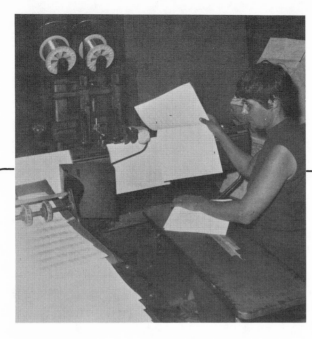

Photos taken at
A & L Bindery, North Hollywood, CA.

Operator opening and placing booklets on automatic saddle stitcher.

Booklets and books of up to 100 pages* can be **saddle stitched**. Wire staples are driven through the back fold of the book as it straddles a stitching table. The book is then trimmed on the open side, the top and bottom. If the book is rather thick allowance for gutter change must be made due to the fanning out of the pages after trimming. Your printer knows how to compensate for this variance.

This room-size gang stitcher automatically picks up folded signatures, transports them by conveyor to stitching heads, then moves the saddle stitched books through a three-side trimmer where they are trimmed and gathered for packaging.

Side stitching is essential on books with a large number of pages and if the thickness warrents a cover or binding tape to cover up the stitches (see diagram). Again, this type of book requires three-side trimming. Some savings

*Paper weight will vary thickness of book.

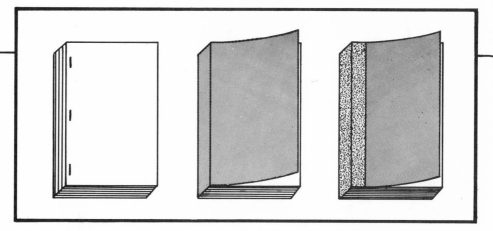

(Left) Side-stitched book before wrap-around cover is applied. (Center) Same book with wrap-around cover glued to back. (Right) A book and cover side stitched together with cloth tape to cover staples.

can be realized here by the advantage of gathered and collated signatures (usually 16-page units). Large magazines are bound in this fashion with covers usually glued to the back binding only to cover up the back of the book where the signatures fold. Side stitched books offer flexibility in the printing since full color inserts of 2 pages or more can easily be placed between the collated signatures.

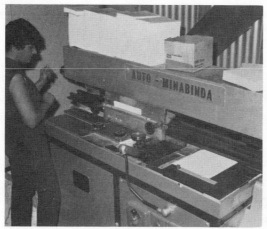

At left the bindery operator is placing a collated book into clamp on perfect binding machine. Center picture shows book being moved across saw blade and gluing wheel. Final picture shows book being glued to cover.
A & L Bindery, North Hollywood, CA.

A newer method of binding thicker books is **perfect binding**. Signatures are gathered the same as in side stitching. Instead of side wire stitches being used the book is placed on edge in a clamp, then passes through a saw blade which roughs the back. It next moves along to receive glue. A scored cover is placed in position for the glued book to move into. Pressure is applied to both cover and book and the quick-drying glue sets in seconds so the book can be removed without delay.

Perfect bound books are very tough, open almost flat, and are relatively inexpensive to bind. Most paperbacks are perfect bound today and more and more magazines are going to perfect binding.

Two types of binding that are popular for booklets and books that must open flat are **plastic** and **spiral**. With either of these methods, books can be printed as single sheets or in signatures which must be folded, collated and trimmed on all four sides prior to binding. Plastic bound books can be very at-

Dramatic views of books bound by spiral wire (left) and plastic (right). The great advantage of this type of binding is the ability of the book to lay flat at any page when it is opened.

tractive since they offer a variety of colors which can be combined with cover stock and printer's ink colors. Pages must be slot punched in a special machine before the plastic binding is inserted.

Spiral binding is similar to the plastic in that the finished book can be opened flat. However, the holes where the wire is inserted are round and are very small. Either steel wire or plastic wire is spiral inserted into the series of holes. This form of binding is rather strong and will hold up well under constant use.

All printing jobs do not require book binding. Simple folding offers a multitude of ways to produce many everyday pieces of literature. There are seven basic letter folds which offer you about any type of mailer, brochure or folder you may need. These folds derive their names "letter fold" from the fact they are letter or legal size and when folded will fit into a No. 10 envelope.

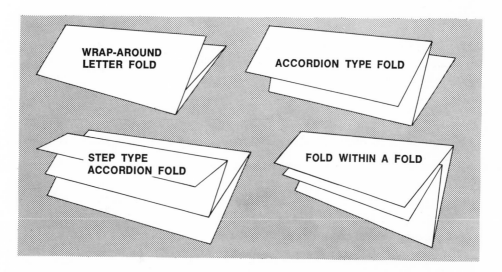

WRAP-AROUND LETTER FOLD—The most common fold such as used in letters which are folded into three equal sections—one section folding over the other.

ACCORDION TYPE FOLD—An ideal method of folding where a headline must be presented at the top of a sheet or where the sheet is 8-1/2 x 14" and must fit into a No. 10 envelope. Folds to look like the musical instrument.

STEP TYPE ACCORDION FOLD—Same as the accordion fold except the folds gets progressively smaller forming steps. Very effective when used with color inks, especially if opposite sides of sheet are printed in different colors and tints.

FOLD WITHIN A FOLD OR TWO PARALLEL FOLDS—Here the sheet is folded in half, then this half is folded in half again. When printed to read vertically, it's excellent for a folder or brochure since it forms several pages.

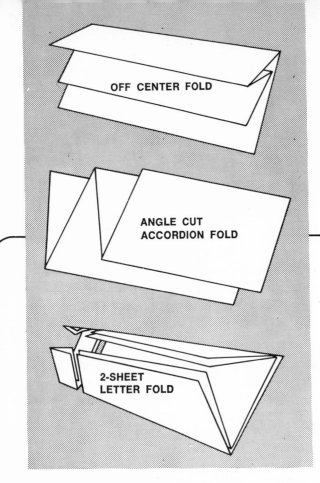

OFF CENTER FOLD

ANGLE CUT
ACCORDION FOLD

2-SHEET
LETTER FOLD

OFF CENTER FOLD WITHIN A FOLD—A variation of the above mentioned parallel fold. Ideal for direct mail pieces, statement stuffers, etc., where the job is printed on both sides of the sheet.

ANGLE CUT ACCORDION—This version of the accordion fold presents a very novel folder being cut on an angle before folding. It creates steps or indices by its unique slant across the folded piece. Very attractive if each side of the sheet is printed in different colors.

LETTER FOLDING A 2-LETTER SHEET—Here's a unique way to eliminate gathering 2 separate sheets together, stapling and folding them for inserting as a 2- or 4-page letter in a No. 10 envelope. It is necessary that it be printed on an 11x17" sheet, folded and trimmed to get two 8-1/2x11" sheets joined together. Some folding machines are equipped to fold and trim simultaneously.

Other bindery operations include hole punching or drilling, trimming, scoring, perforating, padding, round cornering and inserting. In every type of job requiring bindery of any kind, planning for it should be made in the layout stage.

The book binding and folding methods mentioned here should help you in determining how best to bind your next printed job requiring such work. Several suggestions follow which can save you money. Try them!

88   A simple way to hold a direct mail folder together after it is addressed is to have a printer or binder stack them in his padding press and run a brushful of padding compound down the center or in several places on the open edge. After the padding cement is dry you cut the folders apart and they are ready for mailing without the need for staples or gummed seals to keep the open edge closed. This one is a real time- and money-saver.

89   It is not always necessary to have a separate cover put on a pamphlet or booklet. A self-cover is an ideal way to cut costs and still have a good looking piece of literature. The self-cover is part of the actual book. Example—An 8-page pamphlet would have pages 1 and 8 as the outside covers while still having 6 pages of reading matter inside. Printing your self-cover pamphlets or booklets in multiples of 4 pages will also cut costs of printing and binding. Never crowd your booklet, instead allow a few blank pages by using the extra 4-page unit.

90   On jobs of large runs (5000 or more) where you have several sheets of 2-sided printing, consider having them printed on larger presses (4, 6 or 8 up) and folded into a signature. This method eliminates the need for collating them after they are printed on a small press. It also cuts the cost of press make-readies. Plate costs will be about the same or somewhat less for a large press than for a small press where several plates must be made to print the same number of pages. Presswork is somewhat less since several pages are being run at the same time even though the cost of running 1000 sheets is higher. Overall, you

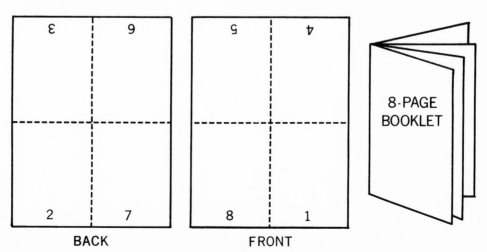

An 8-page signature (printed front and back) which when folded makes an 8-page booklet.

can save on the entire job in printing and in bindery by using this method. You can also save time since the job will require less time to fold and trim than it would take to collate a large number of pages if run on small sheets.

91 Utilizing the French fold is an inexpensive way to produce a mailer or brochure since it is only necessary to print on one side of the paper. Yet, when folded, it gives the appearance of being a multisided piece. Also, lighter stock can be used, thus giving you further savings in paper.

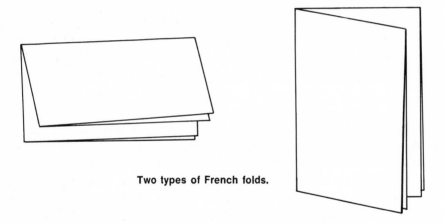

Two types of French folds.

CHAPTER 15

Mailing Pointers

Not all of the printing you order will be sent through the mails. In the literature that is sent via mail service, unnecessary frustrations and wasted time can be avoided by knowing about permits, best times to mail and other pertinent facts.

Up to this point it would be foolhardy to have planned and printed a beautiful piece of literature only to have it mailed in the wrong fashion at the wrong time. Proper mail handling is very important if maximum results are to be expected.

Unless you personally handle the mailing of your literature, it is wise to put some competent person in charge—one who will take an interest in the job and follow Post Office procedures diligently.

A good point to remember is that it costs the same amount in postage to send a shoddy appearing mailing piece as it does a well planned and attractively printed one.

This chapter provides much vital information about mailing permits, best times to mail, state abbreviations and other date.

92 Much time and money can be saved by your office force if you have permits printed on your outgoing mail. There are several types which can be used for various types of mail.

First Class Outgoing Mail—No charge for permit. You pay at First Class rate only for the items you mail. Mail must be taken to the Post Office where permit originates from. Check with your local postmaster for information on this handy permit.

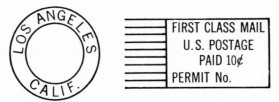

First Class Reply Mail—Most businessmen are quite familiar with the reply card and envelope mail used by many companies. Again there is no charge for the use of reply mail permits. You pay only for the envelopes that are returned to you plus 2¢ for collection. They can be used for regular mail or airmail. Here are examples of typical reply mailers:

The cost of reply envelopes is well worth it. Many times for want of an envelope and stamp a sale is lost. Ask your local postmaster about getting a first class reply permit. It costs nothing.

Third Class Permit—If you are using the mail to make large mailings you should consider the bulk mail permit. It allows you to mail up to 2 ounces in envelopes or as self-mailers for only 6.1¢ each.* There is a charge for a Third Class Permit, plus an annual fee to keep the permit in use. However, if you mail several thou-

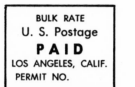

sand pieces annually it does pay off. A mandatory requirement is that all bulk mail must be zip coded and sorted by states, cities and areas. Also "Third Class Mail" must be printed somewhere on the envelope. Of course if you want to use Third Class Mail without the bother of sorting and Zip coding every piece you can still mail 2 ounces for only 10¢* simply by tucking in the envelope flap and applying a postage stamp or metered stamp.

93   Your First Class mail will be forwarded or returned to you without charge. In Third Class mail, it is necessary to print the following on the envelope return if you want your mail returned to you: **RETURN REQUESTED**. If you want the recipient's address corrected then this statement must be printed on your envelope: **ADDRESS CORRECTING REQUESTED**. There is a 2¢* charge for any Third Class mail returned to you.

94   If you use window envelopes, you will get the best results if you mail between the twenty-fifth of the month and the tenth of the following month. People seem to be more responsive during this period if they receive window envelopes that do not contain bills. The difference in the printing cost of window envelopes vs regular envelopes is minimal. Addressing can be done on a letter, folded to fit the window, or on a reply card which you may want the receiver to send back to you.

95   Outside envelopes out-pull post cards anywhere from 60% to 400% and out-pull self-mailers from 50% to 130%.

96   Use letters whenever possible to do so. Letters, when used alone, out-pull any other form of mailing up to 400%. The most important thing about the letter is that **IT IS YOUR MOST POWERFUL FORM OF ADVERTISING**.

*As of March 2, 1974.

97 To help you get more for your money when you mail your advertising material, here is the best time for your prospects to receive your message.

Wednesday is better than Thursday, Friday, Saturday or Monday to receive mail.

Mondays are bad for business people.

When mailing to homes, the day doesn't matter.

The best months to mail, in order of importance: October, January, February, September, March, April, November, December, May, June, August, and July.

The first four months of the year and September, October and November are almost always productive.

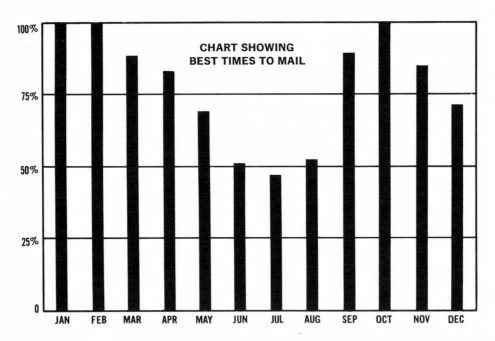

CHART SHOWING
BEST TIMES TO MAIL

98 A description circular or other sales sheet about your product or service will add to the power of any letter. Use the letter to direct attention to the circular or sales sheet. Whenever possible, use illustrations.

99 An order form and addressed reply envelope will always help pull orders. However, a reply card will suffice if you're not asking for money.

100 Many types of printing can be converted into self-mailers to reduce printing, mailing and postage costs. By printing your logotype, address and mailing indicia on the reverse side of your sales sheet or adding an additional sheet to the mailing you can eliminate the need for envelopes on many occasions.

101 The use of the new United States Standard Two-Letter abbreviations shown here can save time and money when used for your mailing—especially for large mailings. Other suggestions shown here will help speed up mail and assure easier handling both in your office and at the postoffice.

STANDARD TWO-LETTER STATE ABBREVIATIONS

Alabama	AL	Kentucky	KY	Ohio	OH
Alaska	AK	Louisiana	LA	Oklahoma	OK
Arizona	AZ	Maine	ME	Oregon	OR
Arkansas	AR	Maryland	MD	Pennsylvania	PA
California	CA	Massachusetts	MA	Puerto Rico	PR
Colorado	CO	Michigan	MI	Rhode Island	RI
Connecticut	CT	Minnesota	MN	South Carolina	SC
Delaware	DE	Mississippi	MS	South Dakota	SD
District of Columbia	DC	Missouri	MO	Tennessee	TN
Florida	FL	Montana	MT	Texas	TX
Georgia	GA	Nebraska	NB	Utah	UT
Guam	GU	Nevada	NV	Vermont	VT
Hawaii	HI	New Hampshire	NH	Virginia	VA
Idaho	ID	New Jersey	NJ	Virgin Islands	VI
Illinois	IL	New Mexico	NM	Washington	WA
Indiana	IN	New York	NY	West Virginia	WV
Iowa	IA	North Carolina	NC	Wisconsin	WI
Kansas	KS	North Dakota	ND	Wyoming	WY

The above 2-letter State abbreviations in all cases have been authorized for use in conjunction with ZIP Code. These specially authorized abbreviations will be coming into increasing usage and everyone should be familiar with them. The District of Columbia, Guam, Puerto Rico, and Virgin Islands are included.

Be sure to use the PROPER ZIP CODE on all mail. Zip codes should be positioned TWO SPACES after state names in both address of destination and in the return address. If the city and state occupy too much space, the zip code should be the last line of the address, positioned DIRECTLY UNDER THE CITY AND STATE. No digits shall precede or follow the zip code on this line.

A Final Bit of Advice

Sufficient time should always be allowed for quality printing. Some jobs are relatively simple and may require only a few days to complete. Others, of the large brochure and catalog type (especially if color is used), can extend into weeks and even months depending upon the amount of work involved and the printer's work load at the time he receives the job.

On large jobs it's always advisable to plan ahead with your printer so he can work your job into his production schedule and assure you a more definite delivery date. After all, he must plan with his suppliers for their services as well as with his own staff.

Put yourself in your printer's place—if you had his creative skill you'd like ample time to produce quality work, too. There's a saying that goes, "Why is it there is always time to do a job over, but never enough to do it right the first time?"

Glossary of Printing Terminology

A/a

Agate line—A unit of measurement used by newspapers and magazines. There are 14 agate lines to the column inch. An advertisement 2 columns wide by 2 inches deep would measure 56 agate lines (28 lines per column).

Air brush—An instrument about the size of a large fountain pen used to retouch photographs and make air brush art renderings. It is considered by some to be a miniature spray gun.

Antique finish—A paper stock with little or no calendering or smooth finish or finish without a shine. Antique paper is bulkier than smooth finish paper. Most books without pictures are printed on this type of paper.

Artype—Complete fonts of type printed on transparent sheets (10x14") that can be cut out and placed on artwork. Hundreds of type styles are available in many sizes from 6 point to 72 point and larger. Available at art supply stores. Also available as transfer letters.

Ascender—The part of type that extends above the upper shoulder of the type. Ascending letters include these lower case letters: b, d, f, h, k, l and t. Type size is measured from the top of the tallest character to the bottom of the lowest descender (g, j, p, q and y).

B/b

Backbone—The bound edge of a book or the part that is visible when a book stands on a bookshelf.

Backing up—Printing on the opposite side of a sheet that has already been printed. Most jobs that are backed up are printed one side one day, the opposite side the next day to allow for ample drying.

Baronial envelopes—A square type of envelope usually used for announcements or more formal correspondence. Also used for many greeting cards.

Bed—That part of a letterpress printing press which holds the type form. When a job is considered ready for the press it is ready to be "put to bed."

Ben day—Shading patterns used by engravers and offset printers to add tone variations—lines, dots, stipples and crosshatches. Named after the man who discovered the process—Ben Day.

Bleed—Printing that is run off the edges of a sheet of paper is considered "bled." Term mostly applies to photographs or solid colors. Extra allowance must be made for trimming photographs or solid colors to the edges, therefore, paper must be printed larger.

Blind embossing—A raised design of letters or artwork impressed on paper. It is called blind printing or embossing because no ink is used. It requires a special embossing die.

Blow up—An enlargement of a photograph, piece of artwork or typography.

Body type—Type sizes 14 points and smaller—6, 8, 9, 10, 12 and 14 point. Body type is used for the main part or text of a printed piece or advertisement.

Bold face type—Type faces that print with a heavy impression. Most type styles have bold face weights in various degrees. Example—Helvetica Light has a companion face called Helvetica Bold. (10 point Helvetica light and **10 point Helvetica Bold.**)

Bond paper—Writing papers are considered to be bond paper. Their surface is treated to take pen and ink. Cheaper grades of bond are made of sulphite pulp while the better grades are made of rags—25%, 50% and 100% rag content.

Borders—Decorative designs in printers type metal used to surround a type form or page. A myriad of designs is available from simple rule type borders to intricate scrolls. Also available in proof form for pasteup (See Artype and Formatt).

Broadside—A jumbo folder type advertisement. It is usually printed on both sides of a large sheet of stock and designed so its message unfolds to its largest sheet size.

Bourges—A variety of colors printed in various tone percentages on transparent sheets. These overlay sheets are used for color separations in art. Also comes in degrees of whites and grays for subduing photo backgrounds.

Bristol—Paper of postcard weight and heavier. This type paper stock comes in a variety of finishes and colors. It is used for cards, posters, displays, announcements and other items where stiffness is required.

Brochure—A pamphlet stitched in booklet form. It usually consists of eight pages or more. A sales brochure usually is a presentation of many facts in lengthy form.

C/c

Calendered paper—Smooth finished papers are considered calendered. Their surface is burnished between the rollers of a calender at the paper mill. Extremely smooth paper is considered to be super calendered. The smoother the surface the finer a halftone can be printed on it by letterpress.

Caps—The capital letters of the alphabet—A, B, C, etc. Often referred to as Upper Case letters.

Center spread—A pair of facing pages. Can be in a folder, saddle stitched magazine, pamphlet, etc. Sometimes there is a space between the two pages. This space is called a gutter.

Character count—The number of letters, spaces and figures that appear in a line of typewritten copy. The count is ascertained to determine proper fitting of printer's type into a given space.

Chase—A metal frame in which a printer's type form is locked for printing. The chase is placed in a letterpress.

Chipboard—A cheap grade of binders board usually used for backing padded forms. It is made from waste paper.

Clasp envelope—A catalog envelope in which the flap is closed by means of a metal clasp. It also has glue for sealing. If used with clasp closed but not glued, contents may be sent third class mail.

Coated paper—Smooth finish paper coated with clay to give it better surface. Comes in dull or burnished finish. Made especially for printing fine halftones by letterpress. There also are coated papers for offset printing.

Cockle finish—Characteristic pucker in paper usually found in bond papers to add a feeling of crispness. Most common in rag bonds.

Cold colors (Blue, Violet, Green)—These colors give the feeling of coolness either in paper stock or in ink.

Collating—Examining the gathered signatures of a book or group of sheets to see that they are in proper sequence prior to being bound. Often the word "collating" is used to mean the actual gathering.

Cold type—This term is used to identify type that is set from any means other than by "hot metal" machines such as a linotype. It includes type set on Varitype machines, IBM composers and other similar "cold type" composing machines including the newest electronic typesetting equipment on film.

Color filter—Some colors cannot be photographed by the printer's or engraver's camera and therefore, must be filtered out by means of color filters placed on the lens of the camera.

Color process—A set of two or more halftones made by color separation. Halftone color printing is commonly called process work. Four-color process requires a halftone for yellow, red, blue and black.

Column inch—A space one inch deep and one column wide is considered to be a column inch. This measure is more commonly used by smaller newspapers.

Combination plate—An engraving plate where two types of artwork are combined on one plate—line art or type is combined with a photograph.

Complementary colors (Yellow and Violet, Red and Green, Blue and Orange)—These three color complements are determined by combining one primary color (Yellow, Red or Blue) with the combination of the two remaining primary colors. For example—Yellow with the remaining two primary colors (Red and Blue) would be Yellow and Violet.

Composing stick—An adjustable three-sided metal receptacle to hold printer's type. It holds about two inches of type in lengths that can be varied from four picas to 42 picas and even to 60 picas.

Compositor—A printing craftsman who sets type by hand or by machine. He must know spacing, type styles, justification and be good at spelling and punctuation.

Condensed type—A narrow or slender type style. This is Regular—A, B, C; This is condensed—**A, B, C.**

Contrasty—When the tones in a photograph are stronger black and white than various middle tones of soft grays the photograph is considered to be contrasty. For good halftone reproduction middle tone photos are preferred to contrasty ones.

Copy—The printing term for the manuscript supplied for a printing job. This copy must be set in type either by hand or by machine.

Copy fitting—Determining the amount of copy that can be fit into a given area of space on a printed piece or advertisement for a specified size and style of type.

Crash finish—A finish put on paper to simulate the look and feel of coarse linen. There are variations of crash finish in different grades of paper.

Crop—Marking for trim the unwanted areas of a photograph or painting. Crop marks are usually placed on an overlay attached to the photo. The printer or engraver follows these corner marks and trims accordingly.

Cut—A common term used for a zinc engraving. The word originated from the early days when cutting was done by hand to make a wood cut of artwork.

D/d

Dead metal—Areas on an engraving not intended for printing are dead metal areas and must be routed or cut away. Also the metal that has been set by linotype or other machines is considered dead metal when its job is done.

Decalcomania—A form of printing put on a specially prepared paper for transferring images to items that would be difficult to put in a printing press. There are both dry and wet type "decals."

Deckle edge—The feathery untrimmed edges on paper stock usually trimmed off. Some special announcements and greeting cards look especially nice with deckle edges.

Descender—Descending lower case letters including g, j, p, q and y.

Direct mail—A method of advertising whereby business is solicited by means of letters, cards and other sales literature sent directly to each individual or firm by mail.

Double thick cover—Regular weight cover paper when pasted together forms double thick cover. For example 65 lb. cover in double thickness would be 130 lb. cover.

Drop out negative—A halftone negative where highlight dots are so exposed that they drop out of sight and do not appear on the finished engraving or offset plate.

Dry brush—An art drawing made with a brush only slightly moistened with India ink. The resulting effect is somewhere between crayon and pen drawings.

Dry mounting—A method of mounting photographs to backing boards by using a dry mounting tissue whose coating melts under heat. A special press is used to heat and impress the photo to the mounting board.

Dummy—A preliminary layout of a printed piece made to the exact size of the same stock as the finished job will be. It may be elaborately done or roughly done according to the customer's needs.

Duotone—Printing a black and white photograph by making two separate plates —one to be printed in a color tone, the other in black. The purpose of a duotone is to add softness and color tone to a picture at low cost.

Duplicator—An office machine that reproduces printing. It can be a mimeograph, hectograph, multigraph or multilith type.

E/e

Editing—Carefully polishing up copy before it goes to the printer or typesetter. Punctuation, grammer and consistency must be followed if good copy is to be had.

Eggshell paper—A rough surface book paper that has the basic texture of the shell of an egg.

Elite—The smallest size of type on a typewriter—12 characters to the inch as compared to 10 characters for pica type.

Electrotype—A duplicate cut of an engraving or typeset form or both made by taking a wax impression of the original. By means of the electroplating process copper is deposited on the wax mold, after being stripped from the mold the copper is backed up with lead, trimmed and mounted on a block of wood type high for printing.

Em—The square of a type size. The em space of 10 point type is 10 points square.

Embossing—Producing raised designs or letters on paper and other material by means of matching dies. Sometimes done with ink, other times without, as in the case of blind embossing.

En—One-half the square of a type size. The en space of 10 point type is five points.

Enamel finish paper—Coated paper made to take letterpress halftone engravings of fine screens. The smoother the coating the finer the screen that can be used.

Envelope stuffer—A small circular for inserting into statement envelopes or other mailings without adding to the cost of the postage.

Engraving—The term used for a zinc cut of artwork. Also refers to genuine engraving process of printing (see gravure).

Etching—The process of acid eating away the unwanted parts of a printing engraving "cut."

Extended type—Any type face that is wider than regular width type. Example—News Gothic Extended, Hellenic, Cheltenham Wide and Craw Clarendon are all extended type faces.

F/f

Fake process—A method of reproducing full color printing by the artist separating colors prior to camera shooting. It is done by making an overlay of each color desired over the original black and white basic artwork.

Family of type—Consists of several type weights and widths of a particular type style. Example—Futura Light, Futura Medium, Futura Demi-Bold, Futura Bold and Futura Extra Bold in Regular, Condensed and Italic would be considered a family of type.

Flat—A sheet of opaque orange paper which contains the negatives of an offset printing job stripped into one basic unit. A separate flat is required for each color of a color printing job.

Flush—When type is set even on the left or right it is considered to be set "flush left" or "flush right" or "flush left and right."

Flock printing—Materials which are sprayed or dusted on printed jobs to give a velvety or special effect are considered to be "flocked." Instead of printing inks being used, glue or varnish is applied so the flocking material will have something to adhere to.

Flop—Positioning a picture to face the opposite way it appears. It is done by turning the negative over when making the print.

Flyer—An advertising handbill or circular.

Folder—A printed piece with one or more folds in which each section when folded makes a complete and individual page.

Font of type—An assortment of letters of a type face to make up an entire alphabet of CAPS, lower case and figures in various quantities according to the letters most used. Example—A font may contain five A's, seven E's and only one or two Z's.

Footnote—Small typeset notes appearing at the bottom of a page referring to items that appear in the text above by means of asterisks, daggers, etc.

Form—Type with or without "cuts" locked in a metal chase ready for printing.

Format—The size, shape, general style and apperance of a book.

Formatt—Tradename of type printed on acetate sheets to be cut out or transferred to pasteups for printing use. Ideal where large size types are needed. A low cost method of typesetting for the layman or commercial artist that can be done directly on the finished pasteup.

Four-color process—Color halftone printing from three primary colors of ink (Yellow, Blue and Red) and Black.

Free lance—An artist or advertising man who works independently either full time or part time.

French fold—A double fold of paper printed on one side only so that when folded its message appears as a four page folder. An inexpensive way to get a good looking printed piece of elegance since only one press run is involved unless color is added.

Frisket—A piece of paper used on a press to hold back part of a printing job from being printed. By changing friskets a one color job can be printed in more than one color. Used in letterpress printing.

Full color—Also called four-color process when three primary colors (Yellow, Blue and Red) and Black are printed to get the full range of all colors.

Full measure—Another term for having a line of type set to justify or reach both ends of a given length.

Furniture—Pieces of metal or wood in various pica sizes below the height of type (.918") used to space out type in a printer's chase prior to printing.

G/g

Galley—A three-sided metal receptable used to hold type forms prior to being printed.

Galley proof—A proof taken of the type in a galley—usually the first proof of a type setup. Corrections are made on this galley proof before a final proof is submitted.

Gang printing—Several different jobs combined on one press run—either for one customer or for several customers. These jobs are cut apart and the cost is divided among them.

Gate fold—An additional fold used on a catalog or publication which when unfolded makes an additional two pages. It is used where spreads are necessary and the normal number of pages is insufficient to tell a story.

Gather—To arrange book signatures or sections in proper sequence for binding. Also to arrange them in sets as in triplicate invoices and other forms.

Glossy—A photographic print made on glossy paper. Glossy prints are recommended for reproduction for best results because of their greater tonal range—blacks are blacker and whites are whiter.

Gothic—Type that is made without serifs or cross strokes as distinguished from Roman style.

Grain—When paper is made, the pulp fibers are forced in one direction by the pressure of the rollers which get progressively tighter. This makes paper easier to fold one way over the other and is called grain. Grain is very important when folding is to be done on a job.

Gravure—The method of printing by the intaglio process where the image is etched into the plate, filled with ink, surface wiped clean and impressed upon paper. An example of gravure printing is the rotogravure Sunday newspaper supplements.

Gripper edge—The edge of a sheet of paper picked up by the grippers of a printing press. Allowance must be made for this gripper edge of from one-quarter to one-half inch depending on the press being used.

Gutter—The inside margins or space between pages of a book. Also the space between columns of type.

H/h

Hairline—The finest line that can be reproduced in printing. Also a term used in printing for close work—"hairline register" of colors.

Halftone—Process of reproducing a photograph by means of a pattern of dots in varying thicknesses. Light passes through a cross-lined screen onto the film in the printer's camera and the ensuing negative is developed with a series of varying dots caused by the light passing through the openings in the screen.

Headline—The most important line of type in a piece of printing that must tell at a glance what the literature is about. Used improperly the headline will fail to sell the message of the printed piece.

Hickey—A spot or blemish which tends to spoil the appearance of high quality printing. Hickies can be caused by dust or lint getting on the plate or type form, skin from ink which leaves specks on plates and type that when printed leave white spots. Yes, even the paper being printed can have its surface tugged at to loosen particles which will cause hickies. So will dust from powder spray dryers.

Highlight halftone—A halftone where the white areas are completely dropped and not held as very light gray dots. Especially good where pencil, crayon or wash drawings are to be reproduced.

Hot type—Type that is set with hot metal as with a Linotype, Monotype or Ludlow machine.

House organ—A periodical published by a firm or "house" to its employees or its customers. A very valuable piece of advertising when well planned and prepared, and used consistently.

I/i

IBM typewriters and Composer—This company makes typewriters which have characters with unit spaces. For example the "i" is two units and the "w" is five units on the IBM Executive typewriter. Their Composer goes even further with nine units to the letter "w" and simulates printer's type exceptionally close. It even justifies spacing for even lines.

Illustrations—Any form of picture or drawing that depicts a situation, product, building or person, used on printed literature.

Imprint—Putting a firm's name and address on previously printed literature by running it through another printing press.

Indicia—The information that is printed by special permit on envelopes or cards in lieu of actual postage stamps or printing from a postage meter.

Indentation—Spacing in type lines from a margin such as for a paragraph. Sometimes the first line of a paragraph is flush left and the following lines are indented to add extra emphasis.

India—Very light buff shades in a paper, darker than cream color. An easy-to-read color which reproduces line and halftones very well.

Insert—An extra set of pages usually added to a gathered book of several standard signatures. Inserts are usually printed separately and placed in a book prior to binding.

Instant type—Another form of transfer type made up in fonts on transparent sheets used in pasteups. Letters are rubbed off the transfer sheets onto artwork.

Intaglio—A form of printing (gravure) in which the image is engraved into the plate. Ink is flooded into the crevices and a blade is used to scrape it off the surface to keep the top of the plate clean. Under heavy impression the plate is then printed onto the paper.

Interleave—Another term for slip-sheeting paper between printed sheets to prevent blotting or offsetting of the freshly printed work.

Intertype—A competitive composing machine to the Linotype. Either machine sets type in a slug from hot metal.

Italic—The slating letters of type styles. They can be Gothic or Roman. *This is Gothic Italic. This is Roman Italic.*

J/j

Job press—A platen press used by letterpress printers to print run-of-the-mill jobs—business cards, envelopes, tickets, etc. It prints in one even impression.

Jog—To straighten the edges of a pile of paper so that they are even.

Justify—To set type so that both ends of the line will be even like the lines in this book.

K/k

Kerned letters—Type characters that extend beyond the body on which they are cast, the overhanging area rests on the body of the next letter. Kerned letters are most common in italics and scripts.

Key plate—The plate in color work which carries the greatest detail.

Keyed advertising—A form of coding which is commonly used to identify results from ads appearing in various publications. For example, in some ads, "keyed" department numbers are used.

Kid finish—A finish on high grade paper or bristol that resembles soft undressed kid.

Kill—To mark out unwanted copy on material being typeset. Also a term used for distributing or dumping type metal from a form already printed.

Kraft—Wrapping paper made from sulphate pulp. Also used in envelopes for its unique strength.

L/l

Laid paper—Paper which when held to the light, shows a parallel line pattern. It is created in the paper mill by wires bound together at short intervals to form chain marks.

Layout—The artist's blueprint or visualization of how a printed piece should look. Some layouts are very comprehensive while others can be very roughly done.

Lead (pronounced lĕd)—Metal spacing material used between lines of printer's type and linotype. Standard thicknesses of leads are one point (1/72") and two points (1/36"). Leads are made up as strips of metal in various pica lengths and are below type high (.918").

Leaders—Rows of dots or dashes used to guide the reader from one end of a tabular line to another.

Leading—Placing leads between lines of printer's type and linotype is called leading. Leading out columns of type so it is easy to read such as paragraphs, around headlines and captions.

Ledger paper—A paper especially made for record keeping. Used for book-keeping because of its toughness, smoothness and good erasing qualities.

Letterpress—A form of printing from raised surfaces such as printer's type and zinc engravings.

Line drawing—Artwork created by contrasty black lines on white artboard. Pen and ink, pencil, crayon or dry brush can be used to make line drawings.

Linen finish—Paper that has the feel and appearance of linen. It is done by passing the paper between special embossed rollers under high pressure.

Linotype—A typesetting machine with a keyboard from which an operator assembles brass matrices of letters. Hot metal is forced against this line of matrices to make a single metal slug of the entire line of type.

Lithography—Planographic printing or printing from a flat surface by water and ink principle. Also called offset printing.

Logotype—The characteristic signature of a business firm cast into a single body of type. Commonly called a "logo."

Lower case—The small letters of a type font. Example—a, b, c, d, etc., as compared to the capital letters A, B, C, etc.

Ludlow—A typecasting machine where type is cast in lines on metal slugs by means of brass matrices assembled by hand. Expecially good for setting large display type where gang runs are required since repeat casts can be made.

M/m

Machine composition—Another term for Linotype, Ludlow or Monotype setting.

Machine finish—Uncoated paper that has a smooth finish but is not glossy or calendered.

Magazine—A heavy metal container used to hold a font of the brass matrices of a linotype machine. It is made up of channels where each letter of the font is stored. When the operator depresses a key, one matrix at a time is released to be assembled with others. After the line is cast, the matrices are returned to their respective channels ready for use again and again.

Makeready—Preparing a letterpress printing form to equalize impression. In the case of envelopes special packing and cutting must be done to compensate for the layers of paper that are glued together to make an envelope.

Makeup—Putting together type, engravings and other letterpress elements to form a page or group of pages as in a newspaper, magazine or book.

Manila paper—Strong wrapping paper made of manila hemp. It is usually left in natural yellow-buff color.

Margins—The areas left around the type form of a page—top, bottom and sides. Where two pages form a spread the margin between them is called a "gutter."

Mask—A form of a frisket to prevent certain areas from receiving ink or paint. In air brush work artists mask out areas they do not want to spray. Masks are removed and new ones are placed over other areas. Masks are also used to block out unwanted areas in silk screen printing.

Mats—Papier mache type of mold made of type and engraving forms used for making stereotype. Mats are used chiefly by newspapers printed by letterpress.

Mechanical—Another term for a camera-ready pasteup for artwork. It includes type, photos, art, borders, etc., all on one piece of artboard.

Middle tones—The soft grays on a photograph between solid black and pure white. For best printing results printers take great care to hold these middle tones for softness and detail.

Moire—Undesireable patterns made from rescreening existing halftones to make a new halftone. Moire patterns can be avoided by shooting halftones as line art since they already have dots. However, if reductions are made then the dots may close up and the dot pattern will be lost.

Monotype—A type casting machine which casts type individually—letter for letter—rather than on a slug as with a Linotype machine.

Montage—Several photos pasted to one artboard in a pleasing manner to tell a particular story. They can be overlapped, put on angles, cut out in various shapes, etc.

Mortising—Cutting away portions of an engraving block to allow space for inserting type or other engravings. There are two type of mortices—inside and outside.

Multilith—A small offset duplicator press used to produce run-of-the-mill jobs—cards, letterheads, envelopes, forms, etc.

N/n

Natural—An off-white color of paper sometimes close to an ivory or India shade.

Negative—Photographic film with the whites being black and the blacks being white. Negatives are made from line artwork, photos, type, etc. They are used to make offset printing plates and engravings.

Newsprint—The cheapest form of paper made from groundwood pulp.

Novelty Printing—Includes printing on balloons, calendars, pencils, matches, badges and similar items.

Numbering—Printing consecutive numbers with special machines on invoices, tickets, etc. Numbering is usually done by letterpress, although some offset presses have numbering machine attachments on them.

O/o

Oblong—Binding a book lengthwise instead of in the usual vertical method.

Offset—The transfer of a freshly printed wet image onto the back of another sheet of paper. Offset also refers to the term used for lithographic printing.

Onionskin—Very thin writing paper used where space is at a premium for storing. Also used for airmail letters and envelopes where light weight is essential.

Opaque Ink—Printing ink which conceals all colors placed beneath it.

Outline Halftone—A halftone in which all background is cut away leaving only the main subject outlined.

Overlay—A transparent acetate sheet placed over original artwork on which color separations are pasted. The more separations, the more overlays required.

Overrun—Printing in excess of what was ordered. Printers try to stay within 10% of overruns. (See printing trade customs on Page 128.)

P/p

Parchment paper—True parchment paper was made from the thin skin of goats, sheep, etc. It had great durability. Imitation parchment papers are now available made from paper product materials.

Pebble finish—A special finish given paper to add texture. It is made up of a series of fine designs embossed into the paper at the paper mill. Halftones print exceptionally well by offset on good pebble finish paper.

Perfecting press—A printing press used to print both sides of a sheet of paper in a single operation. Such a press must have special drying attachments.

Perforating—The cutting of a dashed or dotted line on printed matter to allow a section of the printed piece to be torn off such as a coupon. Some perforating is done on presses, other in binderies.

Photo composition—Type that is set photographically by hand or by electronic devices from film fonts or grids. End result is film negative, film positive or paper print of complete job set in types and sizes selected.

Photostat—Paper negatives and positives made by a special camera which copies original art, type, etc., through a prism and lens thus producing a forward result.

Pi—When a type form is spilled or gets thoroughly mixed it is called pi. If it is set by hand (letter by letter) then a real mess is involved. Letters of many sizes and faces of types can become jumbled in one pile.

Pica—Basic type measurement—one-sixth of an inch or 12 points. Typewriters using pica size type measure 10 characters to the inch as compared to elite at 12 characters per inch.

Planographic—A method of printing. It refers to the offset or lithographic type of reproducing an image from a plane or flat surface.

Platen press—A job printing press which makes its impression on a flat surface or platen in one uniform contact.

Point—A printer's measure—1/72 of an inch. Twelve points equal one pica. Type is measured by the point system—6, 8, 10, 12, 14, 18, 24, 30, 36, 42, 48, 60 and 72 points being the most common standard sizes.

Primary colors (Yellow, Red and Blue)—The basic colors from which all colors can be made. Full color or four-color process printing must use these three colors plus black.

Prints—Paper photographs made from negatives. Glossy prints are best for reproduction purposes since their reflective surface bounces light for copying halftone negatives.

Process plates (4-color)—Halftone color plates of a printing job. They include plates for yellow, red, blue and black which when printed in register produce a beautiful finished full-color job.

Progressive proofs—Proofs made of process plates in progressive steps to show the results of each color as it is added to the next—yellow with red, yellow with blue, yellow with red and blue, etc.

Proof—Preliminary impression of a type form or a finished engraving for the purpose of correction.

Q/q

Quad—Pieces of type metal, less than type high, used for paragraph indentions, to fill out lines at ends of paragraphs, centering and general line spacing where large spaces are required. It is the square of a particular size of type—a 10 point quad is 10x10 points.

Quoins—This word is pronounced "coins." Quoins are metal wedges used to lock up type forms in a printing chase prior to putting them on the press.

R/r

Rag content—Paper containing a certain proportion of rag fiber, varying according to the grade—25% rag, 50% or 100% rag.

Rate card—An information card provided by a magazine or a newspaper to give rates of space, advertising dimensions, circulation, mechanical requirements, etc.

Ream—A unit of measure for paper—500 sheets of any size.

Register—Accurate superimposition of printing plates in color printing. Each color must register into the next for perfect results. Also refers to correct positioning of work on paper.

Relief—A method of printing commonly called letterpress since it means printing from a raised or relief surface such as type or engravings.

Retouching—Skilled touching up of photographs to bring out highlights and details often missed by the camera. Both hand brush work and airbrush are used for retouching.

Reverse plate—When printing is desired to be white against a black background the plate is reversed by making a film positive prior to making the engraving. Instead of using the negative, the engraver or printer uses the film positive.

Ripple finish—Another fancy finish put on paper at the paper mill. It has a wavy or rippled look to it and prints up very well.

Roman—Type faces with serifs or cross lines. This is Roman style type. Roman style dates back to the days of the Roman empire.

Rotary press—A high speed printing press (letterpress, offset or gravure) which prints paper on both sides from a continuous roll. All rotary presses use plates of some kind.

Rotogravure—Gravure printing from cylindrical copper plates. Used by newspapers to print Sunday magazine supplements and by catalog users where long press runs are required for greater economy.

Rough—A layout of a printed piece without great detail or precision. Usually roughs are made to find the best possible layout idea. Once selected, a more comprehensive layout is made.

Routing—Cutting away of unwanted metal on a zinc engraving. Routing is also used to cut non-printing areas lower. A router is a high speed drill type tool.

Rule—Type high strips of metal in various printer's point widths used to make lines and frames when printed. When used as boxes, the corners should be mitered.

S/s

Saddle Stitch—Booklets that are stitched with wire staples on the back fold are saddle stitched. They are laid open over a saddle to receive their necessary binding.

Sans serif—Refers to type faces without (sans) serifs. Modern type styles include many of these Gothic or sans-serif faces. Some more popular names include—Futura, News Gothic, Alternate Gothic, Univers and Helvetica.

Scaling—Calculating the reduced size of a photograph or a piece of artwork prior to giving it to the printer. It entails figuring widths and heights to fit areas indicated in layouts.

Scoring—A term used to mean creasing heavy paper so it can be folded without breaking the fibers especially if folding is to be done across the grain.

Scratch board—A special clay coated card stock used to get wood cut effects by scratching and scraping away inked areas. Black and white reverse effects are also possible with the scratch board technique.

Screen—A cross lined screen of various number of lines to the inch used to break up a photograph into dots so it can be printed as a halftone. Screens vary from 65 to 133 lines to the inch.

Screen angle—The angle to which two or more halftone screens are turned with relation to one another to avoid the making of a pattern.

Script—A type face which looks like writing. There are formal and informal scripts in many different weights.

Secondary colors (Orange, Green, Purple)—Colors produced by mixing two primary colors (Red, Yellow and Blue) in any proportion.

Self-cover—Some booklets do not warrent the need for a cover stock heavier than paper inside. Therefore, the same paper is used to form a cover and this is called a self-cover.

Self-mailer—A printed piece designed to be mailed without an envelope.

Serif—Type style with cross lines referred to as Roman.

Series of type—All the sizes of a particular type face make up a series. For example—Futura Medium in 6, 8, 10, 12, 14, 18, 24, 30, 36, 48, 60 and 72 point sizes would constitute a series in that type face.

Shade—Adding black to color gives it a shade.

Signature—A number of pages printed on one sheet of paper that are folded to form a signature of pages in sequence. Several different signatures when gathered make up a book which is then bound.

Side stitch—One method of binding a book along the left hand side through the signatures is side stitching or stapling. A cover of some kind is generally put on to cover up the stitching prior to trimming.

Silk screen printing—A method of printing through a stencil attached to a piece of silk stretched over a frame. Signs are excellent examples of work produced by silk screen printing.

Slip sheeting—Inserting sheets of paper between freshly printed sheets coming off the press to prevent offsetting of ink onto the back of previously printed sheets.

Slurred—A fuzzy or imperfect impression made by indirect pressure. To be avoided if quality work is desired.

Small caps—Capital letters of a type font lower than normal capital letters. Small caps are used to emphasize a word or words without using the overpowering strength of full size capital letters. Small caps are usually stronger than upper and lower case italics.

Spaces—Fine pieces of type metal less than type-high for spacing between words. Very thin spaces of one-half and one point are used to letterspace if required.

Speedball pens—Special lettering pens used to make posters and signs. They come in a variety of widths and points so various type styles can be lettered.

Square finish halftone—A rectangular halftone not necessarily square. Different than an outline halftone in that the background is left on.

Stereotype—A duplicate printing plate made from a paper mold of the printed type setup. Many newspapers still print from stereotypes wrapped around rotary press cylinders.

Stet—A proofreaders mark meaning "let it stand." Crossed out material which is to be left in copy should be marked with the word stet.

Stripping—The art of positioning negatives in offset flats from which plates are made. Small pieces of scotch tape are used to hold the negatives to the opaque flats.

Substance—A basic weight used to measure paper. A given size of paper is based on ream (500 sheets) weight. Example—500 sheets 25x38"—70 lb. paper.

Sulphite paper—Paper made from harder woods, pine, spruce, etc., by the sulphite process with sulfuric acid.

Super calendered—A high finish put on paper to make letterpress printing of photos better. Super calendered paper does not exceed enamel paper.

Surprinting—Placing tones over printing areas to get special gray backgrounds. Surprinting must be handled with care or reading matter can be obliterated.

Swash letters—Capital letters having extra flourishes used for ornamental purposes.

T/t

Tertiary colors—(Yellow-Orange, Orange-Red, Blue-Green, Yellow-Green, Red-Violet, Blue-Violet, etc.)—These colors are produced by mixing any two secondary colors which are the result of mixing two primary colors.

Text paper—A better grade of rough surfaced printing paper used for books, folders, programs, etc., where artistic effects are desired.

Thermography—Raised printing resembling genuine engraving. It is accomplished by sprinkling a special powder over a freshly printed image, then heating the paper it is printed on. The result is a raised surface of printing.

Three-color process—Printing is done the same as in four-color process except black is eliminated.

Tint—Altering colors of ink by adding white to get soft hues.

Tint block—A printing block used to print solid or tint colors as background over which type or pictures are printed in black or in a stronger color. Tint blocks can be made of rubber, linoleum, zinc, plastic or copper.

Tone—The variation of a color. A black and white photograph has middle or gray tones.

Trademark—Any device which identifies the origin of a product, or the organization which makes it. It can be a symbol or a name or both.

Transparent ink—A printing ink which does not conceal nor seriously modify the color beneath. Transparent ink allows the under colors to show through. Process colors are transparent so they'll blend to form all possible colors.

Transparency—Color prints put on film instead of paper. Paper prints can be made from transparencies. Transparencies usually reproduce better than paper prints.

Trimmed size—The final size of a piece of printed literature—book, brochure, folder, catalog, etc. Allowance must always be made for this final or trim size when printing especially if bleeds are used.

Two color plates—A set of two plates which must register into each other when printed in their particular colors. They can be line or halftone engravings or both. If halftone is to be printed as a duotone then the screens must be angled 30° different so the dots won't cover each other.

Type high—A standard of type measure .918 of an inch high.

U/u

U. & L.C.—Another way of saying set type in Caps and lower case.

Upper case—The capital letters of a type font—A, B, C, etc.

Upright—A book or catalog that is bound in its long dimension as are most books. For example a book 8-1/2x11" would be bound on the 11" side to be upright as opposed to oblong—the 8-1/2" way.

V/v

Varnishing—To protect and gloss coat printed matter such as display cards, book covers, catalog covers, and the like. Varnish can be applied to the entire surface of a sheet by a press.

Velox—A paper print of a halftone used in pasteups of artwork to save negative stripping costs. A Velox print also allows you to see the finished job on the camera-ready artboard.

Vellum finish—Smooth finish in paper produced in the plating calendar and resembling the surface of true vellum.

Vignette—A halftone in which the edges fade off gradually to a light gray or white. In some instances only part of the halftone may be finished in vignette.

W/w

Warm colors (Red, Yellow, Orange)—These colors add life and warmth to a printed job in paper or ink.

Wash drawings—An artist's rendering made with lamp black paint diluted to various gray tones. When applied professionally they can resemble a soft photograph and are often used as a substitute.

Watermark—The brand name of a paper impressed into the sheet at the paper mill. Usually seen best when held to the light.

w.f.—An abbreviation for "wrong font" as used by proofreaders. It implies that letters of type fonts are mixed.

Web press—A printing press which prints from rolls of paper such as for a newspaper or magazine. After being printed it is cut off to proper size at the delivery end of the press.

Widow—The end of a column or paragraph of reading matter which appears at the head of the next paper or column. Sometimes only a word is left to make a widow. Widows should be avoided by more careful type planning.

Work and turn—A method of printing both sides of a sheet of paper in one impression, then turning it over along its gripper edge and repeating the printing to save the cost of two separate press runs necessary for a two-sided job.

Wove paper—Paper which does not have the marks of the wire gauze on which it was laid during its finishing. Wove paper usually has a soft smooth finish.

Wrong font—Letters of one type style mixed with those of another style. Not always easily distinguishable.

X/x

Xerography—A process of static electrically copying an image onto an offset printing plate and then reproducing it onto paper. Special Xerox copy machines can also do this same reproducing without the need of an offset press.

Z/z

Zinc engraving—A line or halftone etching or engraving made for letterpress printing.

Zip-a-tone—A trade name for screen patterns used to create special effects on art work—dots, lines, stipples, materials.

Printing Trade Customs

Code of Practices of Typesetters, Engravers and Printers

ORDERS—Regularly entered orders cannot be cancelled except upon terms that will compensate the printer against loss.

ALTERATIONS—All alterations or changes directed by the buyer or his agent subsequent to the acceptance of the order, are charged additional in accordance with the time and materials consumed therein.

ART WORK, SKETCHES, DUMMIES, LAYOUTS, ETC.—Submitted with estimates, are considered as having been made upon order and are charged additional in accordance with the time and materials consumed therein.

PROOFS—If proofs are submitted to the customer, corrections, if any, are to be made thereon and the proofs returned to the typesetter or printer marked "OK", or "OK with corrections", and signed with the name or initials of the person duly authorized to pass on same. If **revised proofs** are desired, request must be made when proof is returned. The typesetter or printer is not responsible for errors if work is completed as per customer's OK.

CUSTOMER'S PROPERTY—All pasteup, drawings, photographs and copies used in the making of photoengravings, or lithographic negatives and plates, are received, held and returned at the owner's risk and the engraver assumes no responsibility for loss or damage thereto beyond reasonable care. Paintings, copies and merchandise of value should be insured by the owner and at his expense.

PROGRESSIVE COLOR PROOFS—Progress Proofs furnished by the photoengraver or printer, show the colors used and the sequence of printing upon paper stocks specified. All changes of color, printing, sequence, or paper stock in the subsequent printing of the plates are at the risk of the buyer.

NEGATIVES—All negatives and positives used in the reproduction of originals are the property of the photoengraver or printer, unless specifically invoiced to the buyer.

PRESS PROOFS—An extra charge will be made for press proofs, unless the customer is present when the plate is made ready on the press, so that no press time is lost. Presses standing awaiting O.K. of the customer will be charged for at current rates for the time so consumed.

DELIVERY—Unless otherwise specified, the price quoted is for a single shipment, F.O.B. customer's local place of business. All estimates are based on continuous and uninterrupted delivery of complete order, unless specifications distinctly state otherwise.

QUANTITIES DELIVERED—Over runs or under runs not to exceed 10% of the amount ordered shall constitute an acceptable delivery and the excess or deficiency shall be charged or credited to the customer proportionately.

TERMS—Net cash, unless otherwise provided in writing; interest charged on past due accounts. All claims must be made within five days of receipt of goods.

(NOTE—The above printing trade customs represent only a portion of the many practices of each of the suppliers listed. They highlight some of the more common points in everyday graphic arts practices.)